TWIGS

The Absorbing World of Church Education

by Gaylord Noyce
with Dorothy Noyce

For Emily, Lee, Rachel, Abigail and Sarah.

TWIGS:
The Absorbing World of Church Education

by Gaylord Noyce
with Dorothy Noyce

Copyright © 1991
EDUCATIONAL MINISTRIES, INC.

ISBN 1-877871-28-1

EDUCATIONAL MINISTRIES, INC.
2861-C Saturn Street
Brea, CA 92621

CONTENTS

INTRODUCTION

At the edge of our vision most of us possess a heightened sensitivity to motion, weak as the view of details on this periphery may be. In this respect our eyes at the edge may out perform what they do by looking straight on. They react to a fluorescent flicker at a desk, the subtle movement of a camouflaged bird, an automobile turning into our path from a hidden side road.

In church education, we need to look from the eye's corner at what we're doing, too. Jesus told the Good News sideways, in parables. That poetic oddball Christian, Soren Kierkegaard, said that trying to communicate Christian truths as if they were outright propositions about mere facts would never stir the soul. Head-on teaching distorted the proclamation of the Gospel. He urged upon us what he called indirect communication. One of the best preachers of our generation says that to catch on to it, we have to "overhear" the Gospel.

Some sideways watching of Christians' growth and their ingrafting to the Christian community may helpfully complement our usually straightforward treatments of program, curriculum, and spiritual development.

TWIGS is a collection of "second takes" and recollections and a few of those more straightforward arguments about church education. Most of these pieces first appeared, over the past decade, in *Church Educator*. Some are new, some from elsewhere.

We publish it mainly for the enjoyment of teachers and church school parents, but the book has other uses too. Many of these vignettes are brief enough, and provocative enough, that they will be useful for opening church education board meetings or teacher training sessions. Allow five to 10 minutes for reading, 10 for discussion; then get on with the business at hand.

Others will use these pieces simply to enhance their own caring nurture of children and their service in the congregation, and well beyond. Whatever your use of them, enjoy them, and let them prompt from you some of your own stories and reflections on Christian learning.

We dedicate this effort to our grandchildren. I say "we" because much of the credit for many of these stories rests with my wife Dorothy. "Dotey" not only remembers; she adds the insights of a school psychologist to the reflection. She could well be listed as co-author, and was in some cases for the original pieces. To her for this, as well as for amazing love and support, I am profoundly grateful.

I am also grateful to Betsy Corsi, Brent Lively, and Carri Patterson for their reports of episodes with children which are included here. There are other former students, too, whose identities I have forgotten. Claire Fowler virtually wrote the "twig" about Megan ("Nothing to Worry About"), and Karlee Etter organized the all church festival I have described. Three pieces appeared elsewhere — "Dear Jeff," "Learning is a Happening," and "Sandcastles," in The Christian Century Spectrum, and United Church Herald, all used by permission. Spectrum was published by the Division of Christian Education, National Council of Churches. All the accounts in what follows, although I have changed many of the names, are true.

ALEXANDER POPE'S COUPLET HAD IT ONLY PARTLY RIGHT.
(<u>Moral Essays</u>*, Episle I)*

"Tis education forms the common mind:

Just as the twig is bent the tree's inclined."

Pope oversimplified. Twigs have their own way about them too. Personalities emerge both from experienced human interaction and from an internal guidance system part gene, part genie. Remembering a child now grown adult, we discover continuities we had never dreamed.

Educative nurture cherishes both continuities and new possibilities present in children and in congregations. Only given such a double sensibility will we keep the faith with a present and living God.

CHAPTER ONE

Twigs

1. BETSY WORKS JUSTICE

Betsy, still only two years old, was playing in the sandbox with two neighbor children. Her mother was indoors, ironing.

Suddenly Betsy burst in, tears streaming down both cheeks. "Boys," she sobbed, "'pank Betsy." "Never mind," said Mother, putting down her iron and picking up the unhappy little girl. "Let's read The Runaway Rabbit." After wiping Betsy's cheeks, she settled the two of them on the couch and began Betsy's favorite story.

Betsy was quiet enough as the story was launched, but then, at the middle of page two, as suddenly as she had come in, she clambered down and, without a word, trotted out the back door. A moment later she sauntered back in, happy, composed, ready to finish the story. "Betsy," she remarked, "'pank boys."

Betsy's sense of outrage was not to be so easily compromised as her mother supposed. Diversion to rabbit stories did not address an innate need for satisfying her sense of justice. Betsy did not seem vengeful, just determined. She was hurt and disappointed by a gross imbalance in her miniature cosmos. Her action seemed not so much a 'fighting back' as a re-ordering of an off-center neighborhood world.

There is in us an inborn sense about human relations. It is something one of our leading political philosophers exploited when he wrote a seminal essay called, "Justice as Fairness" (John Rawls). When that sense is flagrantly violated, something in us creates what we call righteous indignation. This feeling of unfairness can be genuine anger, but it is not even then the same as hatred.

The Old Testament speaks much of the wrath of God, the anger of God, but never of hatred toward Israel. "I hate and despise your feasts," yes, but that is not hatred for Israel. In Hosea, Yahweh speaks for nearly 10 chapters of Israel's injustices, and of punishment, but then very tenderly makes promises of love. "How can I give you up, O Ephraim?...My heart recoils within me...I will not execute my fierce anger." (11:8,9)

Healthy children, unless unduly intimidated by a chaotic and violent environment, possess an astounding initiative and selfhood. Part of that, as they begin to move from isolated and then "parallel play" to interaction with others, is a latent sense of fairness. As we nurture them toward the grown-up non-violent ability to let insults go without retaliation, we need nonetheless to cherish their sense of selfhood. We can celebrate their sense of proportionate justice, even in the form of petty quarrels and some righteous indignation. We learn this from the pacifists, with a second look. Gandhi's non-violence was not passive. It was a militant pacifism, employed in justice-seeking. So too was Martin Luther King's. The rabbit story diversion failed to honor justice; it left something unfinished in the sandbox episode, like an unresolved musical dissonance waiting for the final chord.

St. Paul speaks as a disciple, one obedient to the Sermon on the Mount. He preaches non-violent maturity, like that of Jesus. "Bless those who persecute you," he says. "Repay no one evil for evil." "Never avenge yourselves." Give food to the enemy who hungers. Overcome evil with good.

Nonetheless, these comments came from a man who could be passionately indignant, even angry, in obedience to the Gospel. No wimp, he could rage against those who subverted his budding churches. "I wish those who unsettle you would mutilate themselves." (Gal. 5:12) He can scold and plead. "O foolish Galatians! Who has bewitched you...?" Paul, like Jesus, modeled full-blooded humanity.

Diversion proves a useful ploy for both parents and teachers. Most squabbles do not warrant philosophy. However, helping a child know that we understand his or her justified resentment is important, helping the child know that we too care.

In our family we enjoy re-telling the story of Betsy's sandbox exchanges with the "boys." Betsy took care of her own dilemma, using her own young power and imagination. She was not beaten down. She grew up without more violence, but with a strong and loving poise as a faithful human being. The spirit evidenced when, age two, she 'panked the boys, was evidently part of it.

THE KALEIDOSCOPE on our coffee table shows me patterns of color and form that change with every shift of my hand. I am fascinated, childlike.

Children have their own kaleidoscopic vision for looking at the world. Letting them cherish, and sometimes share, their perceptions of the amazing world around them, and showing our interest, we nurture their spirit. It may be a covered place beneath a tree, a hermit crab in its borrowed home, or a whitened rib that we admire with them, of a long-dead dog or horse from a deserted sunny meadow. It may even take a little stretching, this appreciation, but it does wonders too.

Interest in what fascinates children strengthens their curiosity. But more than that, it prompts self-images of explorer, inventor, or naturalist, these grandiose fantasies, some of which we all need for growing.

"Reinforcement," the psychologists call it — affirming good behavior, which leads to more good behavior. But it may do far more, leading to new self-understanding.

2. KATHIE LEARNS WHO SHE WAS TO BE

To this day, Kathie remembers a time, 30 years ago, when she was but three. Kathie was part of a large extended family, one that included her mother and father and their eight brothers and sisters, and all their children, Kathie's many cousins. All eight families lived near-by. Virtually any time Kathie's family visited Grandma's house on the other side of town, uncles and aunts and cousins were also there.

The three-year-old time Kathie talks about she found her Uncle Roger alone in the living room. Roger was a man who was socially ill at ease, a nongregarious loner. In this respect Roger was different from all the other uncles and aunts.

Unaware of all that, when Kathie came upon Roger, all she took note of was an empty lap, and Kathie immediately climbed up on it. To three-year-olds, that's what laps are for.

Coming into the room right then, Kathie's mother saw the episode. Later, in the car going home, she commended Kathie by telling Kathie's father. "Wasn't it something that little Kathie saw Roger was alone and lonely, and went to be with him?"

Kathie writes of that incident and how it formed her, "I was praised for my behavior, and, for better or worse, I started down the road of taking care of others. I began to put their needs and wants above my own. The simple act of climbing into my uncle's lap was seen not as an individual act, but as a sign of who I was."

MY NEW PEAR TREE IS THRIVING, and I've learned to shape it with little struts notched at the ends. I adjust them to hold the youngest shoots out horizontal so they grow into useful branches, away from others.

That doesn't make me a creator of my tree. I have to count on the young tree's inner vitality and on rain and soil and sun. Children too need our guiding nurture, but they emerge from the womb with styles of their own. In fact one child may kick and move restlessly, and exubrantly, during the whole third trimester of pregnancy, while a sibling to be, during another pregnancy, shows far more restraint. I refuse to bend my pear twigs without a sense of their own tendencies. We do better to capitalize on children's initiatives than to bend young enthusiasms so forcibly that we squelch the essential energy behind constructive self-direction.

3. NO PHONY COVER-UP FOR KAREN!

Karen, three years old, was in a season of rebellion. She complained. She continually said "No" instead of "Yes." She pouted. She lived, as her parents remember it, from tantrum to tantrum. Worst of all, she whined through most of her meals.

One evening as the family paused for a unison grace at dinner, Karen chimed in with the familiar, resentful whine. She knew non-participation was frowned upon but she could get her feelings out in her manner of speech anyway. "Bless the Lord, and forget not all God's benefits." Four pleasant voices, plus Karen's wail.

Dad stepped in, "Karen, that didn't sound very thankful." And Mom answered Dad, trying to move on with the meal, "Well, I'm sure it was meant thankfully."

Dinner proceeded, Karen glum and silent. For perhaps five minutes, her food untasted, she sat and glared. Then came a burst of indignation: "Mommie," scolded Karen, "just don't you say another word. 'Cause you know very well that was not meant thankfully!" The words were articulated in near baby-talk accent, but the meaning was clear. Karen would not allow a phony cover-up.

Moral integrity is a subtle virtue in children as well as in adults. It does not equate with altruism or with an out-going personality. We may do better by calling it authenticity. Karen was not about to be satisfied with a well-meaning attempt to reinterpret her unhappiness. That was to rob her of her strongly held resentments, and they were part of who she was. It was an adult trick, this theft. Far better, in hindsight, a different response. Mom might have said to Dad, instead, "Karen's voice irritated me too. Karen, I think, is angry about something. We can ask her about that, or we can go ahead and eat. What do you think?"

We all know people who are pleasant, but in a phony way. We don't seem to know them as persons, only as a facade, a front. Underneath there may be a person, with passions, anger, distrust, generosity, and convictions, but they are covered up because of the person's well-bred misapprehension that pleasantries are kinder and more proper. Some would even make them out to be more Christian. Kindness is no doubt a Christian virtue, as are love, joy, peace and long-suffering. So too, however, is authenticity. Karen somehow knew this, even at the age of three.

The same St. Paul who wrote about love and joy and peace is credited in Ephesians with advising, "Be angry, but do not sin." The same Jesus who preached the Beatitudes and argued for turning the other cheek and going a second mile drove physically from the sacred temple courts the moneychangers. Martha and Mary and Peter all come across likewise as outstandingly authentic people, not actors pretending or parading sweet personalites as virtue.

In teaching our children, we have a paradoxical assignment. We want to show them a better way than resentment and anger and downright meanness to their fellows. At the same time, we do not want them to adopt a peaceable manner merely as a phony cover-up. We honor, that is, the openness and honesty of real feeling. In arguing for the exuberant freedom of Christian experience, and against faint-heartedness in faith, against a kind of timidity that undercuts vigorous commitment to God's righteous but forgiving will, Luther said once, "Sin boldly."

Sometime after Thanksgiving every year, in spite of cheap long-distance rates, we still write an annual Christmas letter. Over the years, we hope we've learned to do it better. When everything sounded upbeat and making progress, sweet and well-lit, there was an artificial ring to those letters. Because they ignored the darker, more confusing sides of our living, they lacked texture. Those dark sides remain, and cover-up is a false approach. Karen and her siblings have helped us learn that with their own young integrity. Karen began to teach us that when she was only three. "Don't sell me short with a cover-up," she would still say, I'm sure, and now she's over 30. As we admit the depths as well as the heights in our humanity we follow a way toward both integrity and the healing of our mortal brokenness.

SOMETHING SAD CAN happen to young children. As kindergarteners they can enter our schools, especially in the inner city or Appalachia, delightfully alive and happy, only to be found four or five years later glum and expressionless, worn down by oppressive forces of poverty, or of chaotic life at home or among their playmates. Their initiatives haven't been celebrated and approved.

I think of this spontaneity as something grounded in the whole cosmos. The laws of thermodynamics assert that all things run down. Higher temperatures and pressures gradually dissipate. And yet the whole evolution of life on earth is not toward the plainer and the simpler but toward the more complex. There is a powerful spontaneity deep down in things, ever sprouting anew as one generation gives way to the next.

One of our tasks is to listen for it — in our children, in ourselves.

4. LISTENING FOR THE INNER CHILD

Reading one of psychiatrist Robert Coles' delightful and moving books, The Moral Life Of The Child, (Atlantic Monthly Press, 1986) prompted several moods in me: awe at the mystery of the developing inner world of a child's life; frustration, and even anger, at the way we psychologize away, in our behavioral 'sciences,' the unique quality of each child one by one; watchfulness, lest in my own fascination with such researches, I forget the holy and the human.

You and I are grateful for those appendices in the teachers' manuals, of course, the ones that tell us what the abilities of this age group and of that one are. Some children need stories; they don't yet think conceptually the way their older brothers and sisters can. Some need play and activity; some can sit still a little longer, and can read. But how often our psychological pedagogy misses so much of the point!

Early in his account, Coles confesses part of what stood in his way, blocking a more insightful understanding of Ruby Bridges, the six-year-old who figures first in this book. Ruby is the little black girl who for months went to a 'white' school in the early days of desegregation in the South, escorted by federal marshals through ranks of menacing hecklers. Says Coles, "I kept wanting to fit what I was learning into what I had already learned...in order to say 'yes' once more to the psychological theory I'd acquired..." His theories would tell him Ruby should soon break down, that her statement about praying for those who threatened her was "imitative behavior," copied mindlessly from an adult maxim of some sort. The theories are wrong, Coles concludes. He comes round, after knowing Ruby and the many children he has worked with over the years, to acknowledge the spirited moral energy in their inner struggles, and, often enough, a mind-boggling integrity.

Coles has an advantage over us, of course, in discovering the inner strengths of children. He is trained as a listener beyond our skills, and he has hours and whole days to spend with a single child in his research. But we can learn from him.

In terms of this moral life in children, what we chiefly need to realize is that these childhood reflections come on their own terms. That is where we so often miss the connections. Coles invites children to tell him about the movies they see, and they see differently. They may focus on a tiny episode in A Raisin in the Sun, not on the big issue of integration and racial justice but on how a mother ought and ought not to teach and discipline her daughter. In To Kill a Mockingbird, instead of the courage of a heroic lawyer/father, a child celebrates the good character that his children find emerging from what had been a strange and scary neighbor.

We may easily dismiss young children as lacking moral insight. After all they can't think as yet on the third or fourth "levels" of ethical reasoning in the "what if" cases Lawrence Kohlberg uses when he schematizes 'moral development.' Or we may criticize teen-age children as amoral because they don't seem to cherish our standard values. Coles helps us recognize a different selectivity in these kids, but one with a passion and moral dignity all its own. While we are preoccupied with hard work and American competitiveness on the economic scene, our children may be passionate about animal rights. While we worry about the sexual revolution and the divorce rate, a child spends a month fretting about phoniness in his friends. We are earnest about housing for the poor; a 10-year-old takes note of a lonely boy in the lunch room. Small wonder, if we adults think and question only in terms of our own concerns, that we find the younger folk so uncommunicative. Small wonder, if there is so little understanding between us, we think them to be "amoral."

Coles teaches us to listen to children and youth in their own language, and not to force their words into our cubbyholes. Reading him, I think I can do a better job of teaching. I will do a better job in conversations with the young. I'm going to let them teach me about their fascination with the Star Wars chronicles, their rock music and its writers, their MTV videos, their pets, their siblings, their sense of right and wrong in school.

Robert Coles shows us courage in a six-year-old which surpasses that of most adults. He shows us a 14-year-old's bigoted hatred being converted into a courageous sense of justice upon seeing a lone black student harassed by other whites just like himself. He depicts a 10-year-old Rio slum dweller's integrity that will not steal or deal, even when it would mean he could bring in money for bread that otherwise is not there.

Kids do have long, long thoughts, if we can listen patiently enough to let an inner child speak out. Writing later of his growing convictions in The Spiritual Life of Children (Houghton Mifflin, 1990), Coles remembers an eight-year-old, a black child in North Carolina in 1962, speaking of entering a newly desegregated school:

> "I was all alone, and those (segregationist) people were screaming, and suddenly I saw God smiling, and I smiled...A woman was standing there (near the school door), and she shouted at me, 'Hey, you little nigger, what you smiling at?' I looked right at her face, and I said; 'At God.' Then she looked up at the sky, and then she looked at me, and she didn't call me any more names." (p. 19-20)

BENEATH THE SURFACE of a tidal pool, well lit by midday sunlight streaming down on the rocky shoreline, I could see nothing unusual as we walked by. The children, however, were fascinated by the colors, and they knelt for a closer view. I was forced to follow suit.

Still, I saw little of interest, but waiting, letting my eyes adjust to the depth and subtle color tones of that underwater diorama, the tide pool came to life. The children saw much of the life before I did — hermit crabs, waving sea anemone, scurrying and swimming infant creatures of half a dozen species.

As with that tidal pool, so with children. Patience is rewarded by self-disclosures, sometimes of remarkable perceptiveness.

5. GETTING NEXT TO CHILDREN

The two things happened within a week of each other. We're meant to learn from such juxtapositions, I'm convinced. That week in eight-year-old Sarah's life, at least, warrants reflection.

First, there was the children's sermon! The pastor in Sarah's rural church started off on the wrong foot by saying a nectarine was a cross between a pear and a plum. "A peach and a plum," Sarah spoke up. Well and good. The story went on about how moths lay eggs on the flowering trees and that when the eggs hatch the fruit has a worm in it. "Now, farmers know how to spray the flowers, so we don't have worms in our nectarines any more." Sarah piped up again: "No, now we have dead worms in our nectarines."

Sarah's mother wrote that the congregation laughed and that "the pastor was a little non-plussed."

Who wouldn't be? That wasn't in the plans. The analogy was breaking down. What the Reverend Mr. Johnson was getting into was meant to be something about getting rid of sin. Sarah displayed the impeccable literalistic logic of her age-group. The teaching completely escaped the children, at least those Sarah's age and younger. Not only is sin an abstraction; for children, the analogical method of instruction is far fetched as well.

Erasing analogies from our teaching with children may seem to leave us with very little to go on, but another conversation during Sarah's week may provide a significant clue to a better way. Children aren't innocent of the same serious emotional and moral complexities in which we all need God's help.

Her mother writes on: "Sarah confided in me she thought the teacher was choosing her to do too many things at school. 'You're afraid it might make the other kids feel bad,' I said. 'Tell your teacher that; you can talk to her about it.'" But how does the story end? Sarah thought quietly a moment, then frowned. "Well," said Sarah, "I kind of like it, too."

Now that is human existence in a day of Sarah's life! Mr. Johnson and you and I need to find ways to get next to that! Sarah has her own pride, her own grief, her own joy and sorrow, her own conflict of egoism and altruism. She and her classmates, just like us adults, know love and hate, disappointment and jealousy and rage. They hurt.

They need caring, affectionate friends, and the forgiveness of sin, just as you and I do. The cast of characters is a little different in their stories. The scale is different — a tricycle damaged, instead of an automobile, a birthday party missed because of sickness instead of an interview for a new job. But the essentials are the same.

Somehow we need to get close enough to our children's lives to translate our Christian sensibilities into their language as we teach. Even with grown-ups, those analogies don't work as well as real-life encounters of affection and personal understanding do. With children, they work not at all.

There's no simple answer to Sarah's dilemma. And there's no simple answer to the adult issue of healthy personal assertiveness and humble Christian servanthood. But for each, that ultimate word of God's gracious acceptance of our struggle to be faithful voids cynicism and despair, and it makes possible the struggle again on the morrow. Sarah and Mr. Johnson and all of us can rejoice in that, without even bothering about nectarines, insecticides and worms.

OUR DREAMS are therapeutic, the experts tell us. In them we work through some of the dilemmas of the waking hours. Unguarded, the semi-conscious mind lets in matters that were kept out and repressed before.

Some of our dreams are nightmares. They can remind us of fears and guilts that are in us but unrecognized or intentionally ignored.

The darker side of human life is deeply acknowledged by full Christian faith. We read of Job. We rehearse the lamenting Psalms. We use the cross to help us worship, and we mark a death with broken bread. With both intellect and heartfelt emotion, we acknowledge sin. We speak of tragedy, and of conflicting goods. We wrestle with the problem of evil.

Children have their own level of insight for the darker side. Too often, the way a dream forgets itself, these insights of children escape us too.

6. ABIGAIL PONDERS EVIL

Abigail was only six, but a trifle precocious in her thoughtfulness. We were driving along a back road in southern, rural Alabama, past a small chicken farm, almost hidden among scrubby trees well back on otherwise rather barren land.

Abbey's mother, who was in the front seat, told us the man there raised roosters, trained and bred for cock-fighting. "What's cock-fighting?" asked Abigail. We explained, mentioning its deadly, cruel viciousness, its slashing knife-claws, its wrongness and its illegality.

Abbey sat quietly for several moments while the gravel roadway kept up its subdued snare-drum roll beneath us. "There are lots of things in this world God made not good," she said.

"Like what?" asked her grandmother, sitting next to her.

"War." Abbey's voice trailed off into quiet thoughtfulness again.

"God doesn't make war. People do that."

Silence again. Then, "But God makes people."

A longer pause. We were seeing other shacks and shanties, other crossroads. Then Abbey spoke up once more. "Gram," she said, "sometimes I get in fights."

Theologians don't ever solve the problem of evil. Abbey's grandmother, in her brief exposition, did as well as most of them. And Abigail came round to our chiefest hand-hold on the problem, all by herself. We are involved ourselves, in our own ways. No one is an island, apart from the mainland of both evil and grace. Confession is as close to "solution" perhaps as we'll ever come. And to the deeper imagery and mystery of our redemption: "Mine, mine was the transgression, But thine the deadly pain."

We adults may need an occasion to point to the cock-fight's brutality, but the children, if there is an Abigail or two hidden among them, can probably take it from there. Our role is midwife, helping the thought — and the confession — find birth. Staying out of the way is as important as encouragement and listening — better, in all probability, than lecturing about evil.

SOME YEARS AGO, a movement called Transcendental Meditation expanded at a logarithmic rate across the country. People were paying hundreds of dollars for being taught simple practices in prayer and contemplation. The success of TM, as it is called, suggests not only that Americans still respond to the new and different; it suggests that we of the church have often failed to teach our own children and youth to pray.

"Teach us to pray," said the disciples. Millions ask it today. Actually, we can see the birth of prayer in children if we watch for it, and it invites our work of going on from that beginning, strengthening it against a culture that doesn't care for prayer.

7. THE SILENT PLACE

Betsy is five. She comes into the house from a quiet playtime out-of-doors in our wooded back yard.

"What have you been doing?" I ask.

"I've been sitting in the silent place."

"The silent place? Tell me about that."

Betsy proceeds to tell us of what amounts to a kind of awe she feels in the sheltered, overhung space between three trees, from which the city noises seem shut out, and in which she has been strangely aware of the spring breeze, the chorus of birdsong, and, although she uses other words, a growing self-hood and her own moments of self-transcendence.

In her own way, Betsy is learning to pray. This is not a cognitive learning — like arithmetic or history. It is not socialization, learning to get along with others. It is spiritual growing up, even at five.

We do not want to disappoint Betsy as she grows. Yet that may happen if we are too narrow with our definitions of prayer. Prayer, most broadly defined, is a conscious-ness of the transcendent, "vertical" dimension of our lives. Thus, it may be the intentional and spoken address to God that we ordinarily think of — the adoration, petition, confession, intercession, corporately or alone in one's closet. However, it may also be a wordless activity, a more passive emptying of the mind, with an emphasis on quietness rather than on speech. Yet again, nourished by the intentional verbal praying and by habits of concentrated contemplation, prayer may also be a consciousness that accom-panies the daily round, a background song or a lively secondary awareness that sustains us even while we are very much focused on the task at hand.

Spirituality is built on all three kinds of prayer, and children need to grow across the spectrum. Lacking that, verbal practice can become too routine, or inappropriate for some intellectual mindset of a later period along faith's pilgrimage. As a symbol of the spirituality of young children, Betsy's experience of the silent place taught her parents a depth of prayer that was all its own.

CHAPTER TWO

Twigs And Branches

Interaction With Grown-up Learners

1. STORIES!

"We tell the stories every morning on the way to the sitter. One of Rachel's favorites is about Granddaddy swallowing the goldfish. We must have told that one five times in a row one morning! Then there's the story of the Valiant's push-button transmission that fateful Sunday, and Karen's nibbled toe a la Wiggly-Nose. Also: tales of West Virginia, the Raleigh compost pile, the rope swing, cook-outs, learning how to ride a bike and the ever-popular Uncle-Tim-and-the-shopping-cart! We haven't even gotten to 'Even a gun to protect us, Boink!' I'm not sure she'd get it."

All that is direct quotation out of an ordinary letter home from 34-year-old Betsy, our daughter, about a daily errand with her youngest. Rachel is but two, and because of a job, Betsy is now spending four days a week away from her. You, dear reader, can only guess at the stories' content, but the process is as old as the hills — and as deeply meaningful as anything we humans do.

Betsy is transmitting a culture; she is sharing excitement, and humor, and affection, and love of life. She is linking her children to the generation before them and the one before that. Later on there will be some other, more complicated stories. They represent other private lore of our tribe, and our tribes — for some are stories that go back more generations, some now from the other line that joined to make this new family, and a few at least anchor us in a much broader historical and social context.

Betsy's letter prompts reflection about our stories. For one thing, we realize that those stories help comprise the little mini-culture that is our family. No one else can understand all the nuances of those stories the way we can. It would take a long time to learn them all. They reveal more of our definition as a family than any external data that tell statistically about our race, religion, income, occupation and location, the way the census does.

That doesn't mean the stories are altogether private. Some of our close friends know a good many of those stories. They have come gradually to participate in them. But it has taken these friends some little time of living with us to catch on to the stories. Some of them, you see, are very brief. Briefer for the adults, of course. We can almost tell them with a phrase and an uplifted eyebrow. A few are about the length of the shortest New Testament parables, as we are taught to call them, which are little more than extended metaphors. "The kingdom of heaven is like leaven, which a woman took and hid in three measures of meal, till it was all leavened."

As a matter of fact, our family stories have helped me understand those parables. The briefest ones like that about leaven may be abbreviations, we think, a kind of shorthand for highly memorable family interactions between Jesus and his followers.

And something else. Our stories are told virtually verbatim, even though they have never been written down. Dorothy's mother told some of them to her over and over at bedtime some 50 years ago, and a few of them had been told to her 30 or 40 years before that! We have an oral tradition, you see, a rich one, and probably you do too. That gives us new appreciation for the crucial way the stories bind us all together and give us roots. It also says a lot about the oral traditions in the family of God.

ONE OF MY FRIENDS virtually refuses to use the word "teacher." Teaching amounts to nothing at all if there is no learner, he says. Nothing is achieved. The word implies education is done to people by others called teachers, and it doesn't work that way. Moreover, morally speaking, if you are of age, your mind is its own. I have no business manipulating it.

My friend's arguments hold especially true for adult education. One educator, taking a clue from European usages, says we have to move from pedagogy to "adrogogy" in our thinking about teaching and learning, depending on the maturity of the learners.

I don't mind using "teacher" to mean a mentor and coach and instructor for children. My friend may be right, however, about grown-up learning. Grown-ups may be better self-taught.

2. SELF-TEACHING'S IMMENSE POWER

In the past 10 years we have seen a wave of self-teaching sweep the country. By the thousands and hundreds of thousands men and women and children have mastered the complex world of home computer use.

Many have gone beyond typing ("word-processing," that is) and even beyond those "user-friendly" exercises to design their own "software" — programs that help with idiosyncratic needs. These self-teachers have done all this in spite of the fact that most computer "documentation" has been about as clear for first-sight comprehension as the heiroglyphics inside an Egyptian pyramid. An entire new vocabulary has crept into common usage: peripherals, print-outs, machine language, bytes, modems, input.

The fascinating part is this: For the most part, the great bulk of this learning, like that of the pop-psychology wave of the fifties or the teen-age guitar-playing in the sixties and the health-concerned self-care movement of the seventies, has taken place without formal schooling, formal instruction. I attended, for a time, a "Kaypro Users Group" in my community, 12 to 20 young and old beginners and near-professionals who taught each other in one of the most informal clubs I've ever encountered. It doesn't take a schoolroom for intense and rapid learning.

We church educators can learn much of importance from all this, and it is worth noting down. First, the most immense resource for learning is not the buildings and books and organizational system and staff we have for teaching but the spontaneous spirit of inquiry, the hungering curiosity for new learning. This means you and I are called to live with an openness to where the growing edges are, where the questions are being asked.

Secondly, we often do best to conceive ourselves as consultants rather than directors of learning. We don't give out answers to questions we propose; we participate in a process through which others seek out answers to their own.

My friend who balks at saying "teacher" describes such a person as a travel agent. A travel agent helps others to know the options and to venture forth on their own excursions. This means that well-publicized church libraries and attractive bulletin boards and a regular offering of guidance to outside conferences and other learning occasions are all part of our central work. Some other metaphors can help. We are architects, or interior designers, shaping environments and contexts in which we hope to find the learners' hungers stimulated, channeled and satisfied.

For me a third and salient clue lies with that users group. Fostering the group interaction of like-minded seekers is unquestionably a big part of our teaching task. Some lay people came to a pastor asking him to teach them Bible. Unlike some graduates of the lecture-room in seminaries, this savvy parson avoided the "I'll teach you" response. He facilitated informal groupings in that parish, through which the group members themselves took turns doing word-studies, reading the commentaries, and prayerfully sharing what the texts seemed to mean for them in modern life. Five years later the congregation had a dozen teen and adult Bible study groups. The church was transformed; and the public library had to buy some extra sets of commentaries!

Finally, if we are to cultivate this immense resource of self-teaching, we have to live with a certain amount of confusion. New waves of human interest and needs arise at diverse points of the life cycle, and vary, intellectually, from science to art to archaeology to ethics in their initial impetus in approaching faith. Without loss, we may sponsor different inquirers' groups that appear to compete with each other: one on the letters of Paul, another on death and dying; one on raising teen-agers in a Christian home, another on the parables. The apparent loss is gain.

The fast-growing early church did not gather to follow an "order of worship" laid out on a Sunday morning bulletin. "When you come together, each one has a hymn, a lesson, a revelation, a tongue, or an interpretation." (I Cor. 14:26) Paul wanted to make sure everyone helped upbuild the church and did not divide it, but he blessed the variety of collegial gifts and the spontaneity.

One church, written up in a little book called New Look For Sunday Morning (William Abernethy, Abingdon, 1975), uses the last 20 minutes of their lengthened and learning-oriented weekly gathering, after worship and after classes, to revive a similar informality. Children may bring a song, deacons can raise up a new concern in prayer, someone shares a moving letter from a member overseas, and there is room for a boisterous passing of the peace among old and young, with hugs in the name of Christ for special friends. Maximum learning and growing, especially learning in the faith, is like that — and we travel agents will reflect that truth. We will capitalize on the spirit's quest in others, provide resources along the way, foster interaction in the crucible of learning groups, and eschew a few of our compulsions for neatness and order.

DOROTHY VISITED TWO NURSERY SCHOOLS, and she was struck by the difference between them. She summed up the difference in an aphorism. The one seemed intent on teaching, the other upon learning.

The difference was evident in the morning schedule at each school. At the first, the children were seated for a lesson on the letter C. Then they were shown a half-hour video tape of Winnie-the-Pooh. And so the morning went. At the other, the day began with play-time, a lengthy period involving conversation with the adults. The grown-ups asked questions about the play activities, leading questions about color and shape and quantity and utility, and about the various imaginative dramas of child-care or road building or space flight that were going on in the room. The goal of the first seemed the provision of information, — to put information into heads; the other, to provide stimulation and environment that evoked curiosity, thinking, creativity. The first came on assertively, "coming, ready or not," as we say in Hide and Seek. The other was more patient, monitoring at a subtler level a child's development.

Children have learned both ways, but the possibly deadening effect of the one, and the apparent nurturing effect of the other, claim attention as important elements in on-going debate in education, whether public or church-based.

3. SHOULD JOHNNY BE LEARNING FRENCH?

Mr. and Mrs. Brightman came into the school psychologist's office concerned for their own responsibility because of son Johnny's high, high scores on intelligence and achievement tests. Johnny was 8, and busy. A Cub Scout, he was also taking judo lessons, and Suzuki violin. He was part of a junior hockey team most Saturday afternoons of the winter. And of course there was Sunday school and catechism.

What the Brightmans wanted of the psychologist was some advice. Did she think Johnny ought to be back in a private school, where he had been before they moved last year, so as to make more of his potential? They knew, for instance, that he could handle more difficult reading material. And yes, he was doing advanced math with two other boys, but wouldn't a larger group of talented peers be more motivating?

Was Johnny unhappy in public school, the psychologist asked. "Oh no," the Brightmans said, "this is the happiest year of school he's had, including two years of nursery. But we didn't want him to get bored." Then, suddenly, "Should Johnny be learning French?" they said.

The psychologist's response helped them think about how children grow, what helps them grow into persons, into real selves. "Every child," she said, "has a right to be bored."

In our achievement-oriented competitiveness, we may deprive our children of something terribly important, the space — those times when we think they might be "bored" — to think some long, long thoughts. To explore an ant hill or a robin's nest on their own. To be curious about something a teacher or coach might never think of. To

25

find out who they are and what they themselves, on their own, most like to do. To dream up their own stories rather than hearing them from television and children's librarians.

There are things to be learned from Headstart. Cultural stimulation at an early age increases academic success and self-confidence in a child. But there is also something to be learned from the Third World village that has no Little League or television; namely, that children can invent their own games and "enrichments" when Nintendo is not available.

Becoming a self and not just a carbon copy of one kind of instructor or TV character or parent is one of the important values we espouse when we think of growing into persons, made as we are "in the image of God." Creativity is another. And creativity, while it builds on learning and training, needs a kind of unpressured leisure, a kind of playfulness for experimenting — with ideas, words, art forms, varied solutions to problems, or inventive melodies, designs, and machines. One of us found the only complicated music he ever composed simply happening in his thoughts in that half-awake state of mind at 6:30 a.m. while still loafing in bed. He was not under assignment from music class at all. Any programmed pressure would have killed it.

We can still learn from that charming little book reminiscing about childhood before the television age, in a family without extra-curricular pressures. The title? "Where Did You Go? Out. What Did You Do? Nothing."

A right to be bored. A right to free time for fantasy and day-dreaming. This too may take some parental supervision and wisdom, such as healthy limits to television watching. The point is that both physiologically and theologically, we know that each person is unique, hardly a blank "disk" that matures according to our programmed inputs alone. Life experience interacts with that growing self God seems to call us to express, and that created self needs some time to digest experience. Children need "boredom", a time when they are not being taught or entertained by someone else but left to discover from within themselves something of a destiny. Postponing French a year or two just might be Johnny's best chance at that.

LANGUAGE makes us human. But language is tricky. In particular, religious language is tricky. We are talking of realities beyond the space-time world that conditions all our speech. To make such a verbal reach, we speak almost inevitably in metaphor, imagery and analogy. Theological reflection and biblical instruction necessitate a quality of depth and empathy in us beyond that of the arithmetic and spelling instructor.

4. DOES GOD SPEAK NOW?

"Does God speak to us any more?" It was a sixth grader raising the question. Jimmie and his new-found friends in the summer church camp class were reading in First Samuel the story of Samuel's call. Earlier they had learned of Moses' call. Diane, Jimmie's counselor/instructor, was not altogether sure how to proceed.

Sixth graders are on a borderline of development. Unlike the vast majority of their younger brothers and sisters, they have begun to rise above literalism. They can somewhat appreciate metaphor and symbol. They can reason and raise questions like Jimmie's. "Does God speak to us any more?"

Diane must first of all be honest. Depending on the way she formulates her own convictions, she may say, "Oh yes, in many ways!" or "Well, not exactly the way the old stories put it, because they resulted from many, many re-tellings, and then they finally came to be written down."

Diane wants to communicate four things to Jimmie and his eager classmates. First she wants to affirm Jimmie in his exploration of religious questions. "Tell me more about what you are thinking," is a good response, or "A good question; let's see what others think." Fortunately, in Diane's case, there will be no hint that children shouldn't raise hard questions with us, or that one mustn't question the detailed facticity of Bible stories. Diane's faith is too mature to let her teaching be poisoned in that way.

Second, difficult as the interpretations can be, Diane wants to share her belief that history is more than a tale told by an idiot, more than purposeless. She believes in God's creative, nurturing presence with the world. God did not, after starting it all going, speak through prophets and apostles, and then abandon ship.

Third, therefore, Diane wants to help Jimmie's group reflect on the variety of meaningful ways we can say God speaks today. Is it clear now that God has spoken to our times by "speaking" to Martin Luther King and Mother Theresa? Is it possible that God is trying to speak to us about our environment, or about poverty and injustice in the so-called Third World? Without dogmatism, providing information as needed and as she is able, Diane helps these junior reasoners think. Because she believes in God's goodness, she will avoid with them assertions that blame God for death and destruction, much as she sees in the world a moral law that often brings on us some kinds of self-inflicted punishment. With her own trust in God's purposes, teaching sixth-graders Diane will proceed carefully when she encounters texts in which God speaks in wrath and promises punishment. For the mature Christian, God is not a vindictive puppeteer.

Fourth, Diane is determined both to respect other contemporary Christians and their ways of speaking about their religious experience, saying "God spoke to me, and God said — (such and such)," and also to honor those responsible folk who know the psychological and theological dangers of private revelations like that. The mental hospitals provide beds for thousands of pitiful souls who hear God's voice guiding them in destructive ways. Jimmie is old enough to think about that. The church has always insisted that communal testing for abrupt new religious experience and private revelation is essential. "Not every one who says 'Lord, Lord'" has God's word.

It was rich discussion, that day when Jimmie interrupted the reading from First Samuel. The class session seemed full of questions, bursting with religious growth. Diane knew it had been a good day and her prayer at the end of class was a heartfelt song of gratitude to God, mentioning among other things, the class' thanks for minds to think the hard questions, and for God's presence. She knew it even more later that week, when one of the slower of Jimmie's classmates, small freckle-faced Gloria, spoke quietly to Diane during sunset vespers, "God is speaking to us now, too."

"EACH ONE HAS A HYMN, a lesson, a revelation, a tongue, or an interpretation." Paul's appreciation for the gifts we bring suggests two more things about the intergenerational processes in the church. The gifts are not brought by elders alone. Children have gifts to share as well.

Secondly, if that is the case, the separate, enclosed classroom isn't the only place for us to do our teaching/learning. We carve our buildings into classroom compartments too much of the time. I have a birch tree that has twigs not only at the growing fringes but all through its internal space. Maybe that's how the church should be, a better mix of the generations.

5. FESTIVAL

One weekend I visited both a small-town county fair and Minneapolis' famed Renaissance Festival. I got to thinking about the common elements that made both so exciting to participants, and about what festival means for learning.

People of all ages were bringing to each event their work to share. To the fair came both 12-year-old Jamie Larsen with his yearling 4-H calf, and Mrs. Olafson of County Road 12 offering her apple cake. To the sophisticated festival came potters and jewelry makers and weavers bringing their various wares. In both instances there were many entertainments and varieties of food and the coming together of friends anticipating the meeting of yet other friends and the enjoyments of celebration. Each was an event, not a chore.

Church participation has or ought to have elements of festival to it. The early Christians changed their holy day from the Saturday Sabbath to Sunday for the sake of celebrating the Resurrection every week.

Undergirding our learning in a good church school are all kinds of subtle celebrative processes. We're meeting friends and sharing our lives. We don roles — not so much knights and their ladies at Renaissance but shepherds and kings at Christmas. We are disciples again, attentive to the Master's words. We're singing and storytelling and absorbing the lore of a culture, not about lambing and better string beans but about patriarchs and apostles and the grace of God in Jesus.

It comes down to this, if my mulling has any merit: How do we think of the lesson plan in experiential terms rather than merely "getting the idea across?" What will Johnny and Susie bring to this little festival from their lives? An account of a pet's antics, or grandmother's illness, a shell from the beach, a new pair of shoes to boast? Can we act out a role in playful learning? (One time at an event in an English park I found myself surrounded by a pilgrimage of kids, each of whom had brought a favorite teddy bear for admission!) Can we laugh with a clown, applaud a well-told story, or sing a ballad? Is there a new taste to try, maybe a peanut butter cookie from the batch one of us baked ourselves?

Current complaints in Sunday school include a terrible discontinuity in attendance on the part of many students. It helps to think of each session in festival terms, rather than only as a part of an ongoing chapter to be mastered, always dependent on the week before. This perspective hints at the need for church or church school worship each week as well as for the content of our learning. Worship is an event — a happening. It is festival.

Our congregation as a whole spent a season preparing for a festival. It was called "Marketplace A.D. 29." We had our storytellers — doing parables. We had our potter, and a weaver. Straw covered the floor in the parish house, and burlap stalls housed vendors and artisans of village life. Zacchaeus came along collecting taxes in denarii from the cardboard coins we began the day with. We sampled mid-eastern foods and heard mid-eastern music. We found ourselves imagining our roles as Jesus' fellow villagers and it helped renew us for being Jesus' disciples here and now in the company of those close friends and far-off neighbors who call him Lord. Fair-time and festival set a good stage for learning.

IF FESTIVAL INCLUDES SPONTANEITY, ritual shows an opposite emphasis. Ritual is the patterned and repeated action we use for everything from brushing our teeth in the morning to praising God on the Sabbath. It is part of children's lives as much as of our own. Remember the mumbo-jumbo of play at jacks or skipping rope, or "Eeny, meeny..." for electing who goes first? Remember "Here I come, ready or not?" Ritual gathers around games like moths in summer round a lamp on an open porch.

6. RITUAL

Mid-October calls for a special trip at our house every year. We drive up into the bronze and golden hills of the New England autumn. We have done it for years — first with our three small children, later with three long-legged teens. This ritual evolved into embellished tradition. Until she closed, we always stopped at Grannie's, a bake shop along Route 63, for a loaf of fragrant fresh bread, and at an Italian's fruit stand to see if he still had roasting ears. The menu always included potatoes wrapped in foil and baked in our campfire along with the corn.

We still go, although the children moved away long since, and we may stop at an inn instead of cooking out. But it remains our ritual, and the kids phone in October to ask if we've done "the trip." When we drive into the hills each year, the children seem to ride with us yet.

Rituals are part of religion and part of everyday life alike. They provide stability and pattern for our living, and, celebrated rightly, they add immensely to life's meaning and zest. Done compulsively, on the other hand, they hem us in.

So give serious thought to the rituals we use at church with children. Think of the children's arguments first, and their significance. "But it is supposed to be this way," says the big sister type, whether speaking of an arrangement of shepherds for the Christmas pageant or of the offering procedure at junior church. Kids under 10 tend to think that rules were handed down from time immemorial by the ancestors and cannot ever be changed. They turn superstitious: "Step on a crack and break your mother's back," echoes this latent fear of disaster if things aren't just so. Mental illness in teen-agers can take the form of compulsive perfectionism in night-long sessions doing homework. "Or else God will destroy the earth," said one panicked 15-year-old who had to be hospitalized.

Thus, our work with ritual is to be done happily, not somberly; it should be done flexibly and light-heartedly. The child who varies the ritual track and "acts up" may be creative, or merely rambunctious, but is not "wrong." I am thinking of the one who runs in the sanctuary space, or even shouts, the one who sits open-eyed during quiet prayer, the one who pouts when the ritual calls for singing. We may want to change the ritual, inviting children to experiment and create new patterns for their common life. But then soon enough we'll find ourselves holding to a new pattern for the sake of stability, which children need, and, in church, for the evolution of a deeper religious sensibility in the midst of it.

With these caveats, we can go ahead to exploit ritual for its enormous potential for good. Let's not leave it to the football stadium and the Olympic openings alone. Few things are more meaningful for a youth group after an evening of fun and games or serious-minded controversy than the prayer circle at the end. And after six weeks of it, how the participants miss it if the leader forgets. Someone else will probably say "Time for prayer circle!" That's the beauty of the 'spozed-to-be-this-way feeling. Think of the hush around candle-lighting, the collective rising up of a congregation at the first chords of the Doxology, the moment of turning to the Bible after settling-in time in the fourth grade classroom, the kindergartners' anticipation when the new book is opened at story-hour.

These are all ritual moments, each of them meaning more than at first appears. In their own ways they help us rehearse life-meaning in an often chaotic and meaning-deprived world. They bind us together, ritual being the easiest way a group of people can organize common action. Being bound together is important to Christians, stressing as we do that we are "members one of another" in our common, caring life. And these simple moments speak subtly of realities beyond the whim of private thoughts or action; they speak of holiness and of transcendence.

WHAT GOES ON within your mind never discloses itself to the extent that my thought can be an absolute facsimile of it. If that is true for articulate adults, so much greater the task of bridging the gulf between my understanding and the feeling/thinking/acting life-process in a child. Before we judge and analyze, we do better to listen, acknowledging the mystery in childhood development and learning, in childhood insights, and childhood courage. Megan's story is a case in point.

7. NOTHING TO WORRY ABOUT

When she was four, in that season of preparation for Christmas pageants, Megan made an announcement as Mom was getting supper. "I'm going to be an angel."

"I know," said Mom.

"But I'm only going to be a make-believe angel."

"I know," repeated Mom.

"Because real angels get to talk to God, and I'm not ready yet."

Megan had reason for her reasoning about real and make-believe angels. Born with severe heart problems, by the age of seven, Megan has survived fifteen operations, six upon her heart, three of them open heart procedures. At seventeen months she spent eleven days in intensive care, given virtually no chance of survival.

A bright and sensitive child, rather than merely suffer, Megan somehow makes her experience a part of herself. She lives with a confidence that baffles her parents and friends alike.

In the hospital once more when she was six, Megan lost a close friend and fellow patient: a two-year-old who died undergoing surgery upon her heart. A short time later, Megan's own grandfather died, and was cremated after a service in the funeral home — instead of in the church. Megan expressed her disapproval.

Evidently taking in all this experience, quite unexpectedly a few months later, Megan asked her mother if she would help her write her "will thing, — you know, that paper that tells people what you want them to do after you die."

Stunned, Mom recovered with a suggestion. "I think maybe we should go talk to the minister."

Megan agreed. She knew the minister as her friend. He had visited her often in the hospital.

After church the following Sunday, before Mom had taken any steps. Megan told the minister her problem and asked for an appointment. He agreed to one, with Megan and her Mom.

Later, when the three of them sat down at the church computer and worked their way through the programmed funeral service, Megan made her choices, including music. The minister made three printouts and they signed them. Megan knows she can change anything in that service whenever she wants.

Megan also chose pallbearers — her father, three uncles, and a family friend. On her own, she calmly called each of these people, asking if they would "carry me when I am in that box."

A few days later, Megan accompanied her mother and Gram when they attended a wake at the funeral home. The minister was there, and he and Megan had a talk with the funeral director. Mr. Smith realized he knew Megan's Dad and that Megan lived not far away. He arranged a visit at her home.

During that visit, Megan put more details in order. She chose what would go in the casket with her — favorite toys and books. She said her parents and sisters should ride in a limousine. When she wondered where she would ride, Mr. Smith, now one of her admirers, asked "How about riding with me?" Later in the week, Megan visited Mr. Smith to choose a casket.

Megan had one more detail in mind. Where would she be buried? Mr. Smith went with Megan and her mother to the cemetary. Megan rejected some plots shown them by the friendly young caretaker for want of a good view, and another because there were no trees. Finally, approving the view at one side, she accepted the young manager's offer to plant a tree. Emotionally difficult as it was for all the adults concerned, the plot was paid for and registered in Megan's name.

All that Megan wanted had been attended to. Megan has never said anything more about her funeral plans. She seems to be a wholly normal cheerful child, in spite of her diminutive frame, her experience, her pills, and her nighttime supplementary feedings through a gastrostomy for her stomach. "What," asks her grandmother, "does she know that we do not?"

After the papers were signed for the cemetary plot, Mom showed Megan the title document and said, "I hope, Megan, you're not planning to make use of this very soon."

Megan replied, "When it happens, Mommy, it happens." — and ran off to go swimming with her sisters.

A child's grasp of meaning in a Bible story, or in seeing a seed sprout, or in meeting death is very much that child's own, never wholly fathomed by the grown-up mind. Megan's confidence, however, and her reach toward others, make foolish any cynic's charge that blind fatalism or blithe optimism are her way of facing life and death.

At one point during the conversation at her house, when Mr. Smith was trying to make notes about funeral arrangements, tears ran down his face. Seeing this, Megan patted his arm. "Don't cry," she said, "there's nothing to worry about."

CHAPTER THREE

Horticulture

Method In Church Education

1. OUR MARVELOUS MULTI-LAYERED MEMORY BANK

Lee was 18 months old already. Beyond "Mama" and "Dada," Lee didn't talk yet. But he spent half his walking, waking hours pointing, and his young mother, almost at wit's end, would name things. Over, and over, and over. It went on all summer. Tractor. Lamb. Window. Cup. Tractor. Table. Rocking horse. Window. Piano. Lamb. Cup. Spoon. Piano. What good would it do if Lee wouldn't parrot the words back, wouldn't talk?

Not to worry. In November, Lee began talking, two words at a time almost from the start, and whole sentences by month's end. All the preceding time Lee had been accumulating data for the marvelous memory bank that is the brain. Now that some other functional systems were operative — tongue and facial muscles, nerve endings, an interior willingness to risk speech, who knows what all? — the words were already available, there in the memory bank.

One of the frustrations of teaching can be the long-time wait for the payoff. We teach so much that seems to go right past the pupil — "in one ear and out the other," we say. But it isn't always so. Much in human experience is absorbed at a level beneath the accessible memory systems of the moment, stored for later use. Lee's marvelous memory bank can give us hope.

Time was, for example, when we segregated the children almost 100 percent from adult worship. The children wouldn't "learn" anything. The words were too long, the service lacked interest. We forgot, however, the storage capacity of the deeper memory system. Children in church can absorb the ambience of worship — the space, the music, the poetry, the stillness of prayer — at levels well outside a verbal learning. They can build a habit of church-going and a sense of being at home with a congregation that may

35

not "pay off" for years, not until after a young adult drop out period, perhaps, a typical decade away from church altogether, or not until a wedding and a child.

Taking children to church requires some patience, gentleness and care. Without that, kids can learn to hate church too. But with those marvelous memory banks we humans possess, they "learn" much more than the big words they don't understand.

Debates over what happens in sudden religious conversions crop up from time to time in discussions of religious psychology. Did St. Paul or St. Augustine, for example, really change that much from before to after their conversions, or was that just how it seemed to them in retrospect? Did their new knowledge and faith spring from dry soil? The consensus, clearly, is that in the pre-conversion period the person was not nearly so impervious to religious influences as it seemed. Some of the message leaked through into levels of memory and reflection below the conscious and immediately accessible stratum. Upon conversion, when the "divided self" comes together, or when the fleeing self turns round and yields, or the prodigal comes back home, then of a sudden, the other memories come into play.

Lee's conversion into speech seemed near miraculous — and that is not a bad name for such learning — but it was not so fantastic as it seemed that great November. Lee was storing up data all summer long. Frustrating as the education of young Christians can be, some of that storing up is probably going on with our students too.

IN OUR CHRISTIAN NURTURE OF CHILDREN we have to trust mightily on a process of osmosis. Faith, as we say, is caught, not taught. We should think of our classrooms as groups of children and their leaders simply coming together as Christians. They are simply going about this regular business of the Christian community, doing the things Christians do together: talking and caring, praying and learning, having good times and working to serve others. We can spoil it by thinking of our classes as places where a leader tells ignoramuses things they are supposed to know. This second view forgets the irony in Mrs. Rabbit.

2. "QUIET!" YELLED MRS. RABBIT

One of the homey sayings at our place comes from an old magazine article, now lost to memory. It had to do with a children's story, I believe, about bunnies who were naughty and making a lot of noise. And then came the words, "'QUIET!' yelled Mrs. Rabbit."

It's the inconsistency that we are pointing to, of course. Someone says through clenched teeth, "That's O.K., I forgive you. It doesn't matter that you just broke the only souvenir we have of that trip to London." And someone will say, "'QUIET!' yelled Mrs. Rabbit." Someone will order another family member to "Calm down! I told you to calm down!" And it's time for Mrs. Rabbit. One of my kids was planning a vacation; "We're going to do some good hard relaxing," she said.

We teach quietness with a quiet demeanor, not by yelling. We teach kindness far more importantly by being kind than by many instructions, harshly enforced, about generosity and love.

Being recipients of conscious acts of instruction is by far the lesser part of learning and growing up. Most of our learning is absorbed, rather than received. Theologian Jacob Firet tells of the person who said to him, in a conversation about bringing up his sons, "Sometimes I say to my children, 'Watch it, boys, or I may have to start bringing you up.'" He knew that his best time at rearing his children was unself-conscious — being a good example of maturity, being spontaneously and naturally affectionate.

Firet expands his commentary on Christian nurture with illustrations of the way self-conscious teaching corrupts the more natural process of ingesting Christian maturity. He speaks of prayer, for example, and how we learn it by being around people who pray. One cannot directly teach a child truly to pray, although one can and should give a child some words. "The father does not pray in the presence of his children in order to educate them in prayer — the thought alone is repugnant," says Firet.

Or think of going for a walk with a child. Far better to go to enjoy the companionship and the walk itself than because "It will be good for the child." Firet speaks of how a child is conceived. We make love for the receiving and giving of love, he says, not in an instrumental way, in order to beget a child. New life comes by the way.

I am one of four sons, who as adults got together only rarely in the presence of our mother. Mother enjoyed listening in on our discussion and our banter. One time, when we had all just arrived and sat down, the opening words came from her: "Now," she said, "Talk!" But it doesn't work that way.

Of course we teach, and we plan our lessons. We think out what we are trying to accomplish. But first and foremost, whatever the age mix and the official purposes, we Christians come together for celebrating and acting out God's love toward us. Where even two or three are gathered, Christ promises his presence. And that presence is a subtle source of Christian growth far more important than our conscious intention and our skill at teaching.

ONE OF THE EXERCISES used for encouraging creativity and doing problem solving is both fun and simple. We model it in small ways when we use a metaphor or simile. Poets and good novelists have mastered it.

I face a problem of storage, and I think suddenly of beehive shapes. That was an actual business solution. In developing a better paintbrush, an industrial committee found help from the analogy of a pump.

Creative solutions follow upon strange, imaginative pairings — social organizations and geometrical figures; thinking process and animals; art works and personality types; colors and moods.

I discovered that classroom process compares well to a musical ensemble.

3. OBOES AND BASSOONS IN MY CLASSROOM

I went to a woodwind quintet concert one evening, and I got to thinking about my classes and seminars and the whole organizing vision of Christian education.

I found help there for our seemingly perpetual educational dilemma of whether to foster individual ego-strength and virtuosity or something more generous and less self-centered.

Of course we want individual learning and competence. The Ninth Symphony wasn't composed by a committee. We encourage individual creativity. In church each student should be learning Scripture and moral virtue, and something of the walk with God. In general education we prod individual accomplishment with grading systems, contests and competition.

But in Christian faith, learning and virtue and piety derive from the covenanted community. Woodwind quintets model covenanted community.

The classroom as musical ensemble! The woodwind quintet brings together a remarkable variety of tonal qualities, and yet at the same time it blends them, capitalizes on them, in just as remarkable a way. Flute, oboe, clarinet, bassoon and French horn. Each child or adult in a seminar or class brings a quality of life, a kind of insight, a life experience that can be valued and that can be complemented by another's. Sometimes people sniff a bit when, in that more classical ensemble, the string quartet, they only get to play second violin. But as the right answer has it, "Without the second violin, all you have is a trio."

The ensemble analogy suggests far more, however. It moves us farther with the entire individualism/solidarity conundrum. Each player is a creative artist, bringing a distinctive contribution of range, timbre, skill and artistry. There are solo moments. But no player, skilled as he or she may be, can be a creative ensemble player without a sense of the broader reality that must undergird and guide the virtuosity — the musical vision of the composer. Together, they are playing one piece. The players serve that collective good, not their own self-expression. By disciplining self-importance, by shaping individual gifts to contribute to the entire musical vision, they achieve their end.

An ideal classroom group has caught a sense of corporate inquiry, or of a collective project under construction. Every child or adult wants to add insight, contribute a panel of the mural, color in a space, make a metaphor. The teacher or the material has provided a sense of the entirety without disallowing the discipline, the tone quality, and the genius of the individual.

Moral virtue, one of our teaching goals, is not based on individual stardom, even on individual moral virtuosity. It arises from a sense of human wholeness. Moral education depends upon a sense of the human reality the Composer has created. We call it a family, a unified community that yearns for the promised Commonwealth of God, and our end is achieved when we find our individual fulfillment within that frame.

The regional musical events of my childhood used to be called contests, and they focused on the winners. Now they are called festivals. The virtuosos still stand out, but everyone has a better chance to identify with the exciting achievements of the entire enterprise instead of succumbing to jealousy. That's a lesson for our classrooms.

There are oboes and flutes and horns in my classroom, and I want not only to hear each one's gift to us but to blend them together in ensemble, creating something not one of them alone could do. I want them to move not proudly away from but creatively toward the Kingdom.

OUR DIFFERENT WAYS OF PROCESSING INFORMATION AND PERCEP-TIONS account for much of the difficulty in making connection between teacher and small children. For that matter, this applies between adults, and among the nations. In a sense every individual and every cultural group lives in a different "world" from all the others.

It is, however, probably a larger gulf between the five-year-old and a teacher, unless the teacher has learned to listen with a kind of second ear, with empathetic insight. There is that commonplace story about the seven-year-old who came bounding in from school with the question, "Where did I come from, Momma?" and whose mother then went into a careful and complicated rapid-fire explanation about conception and pregnancy and birth. The child finally found enough of a break in all the multisyllable talk to blurt out, "I mean where did I come from? Janie says she came from Detroit! Where did we come from?"

Joyce Carol Oates portrays a five-year-old and her mother in similar conversation, but with insight that probes the depths of existential mystery like that of any adult who wonders what self-consciousness and the human soul and birth and death themselves are all about. The five-year-old asks the same question. With simple and sensitive language at first, this patient and empathetic mother speaks of how it was to be expecting, and of the impatient full-term baby and the birth canal and Susan's entry into the world. The mother had missed the question's overtones about the mystery of selfhood, however. Susan is unsatisfied, and the scene finally turns petulant on both sides as Susan asks, at least for the 25th time, "Yes, Mother, I know, but where do I come from?"

4. WHAT'S GOING ON HERE?

"When I see a mistake in arithmetic," said a teacher, "I ask myself 'What's going on here? How did that answer come about?'"

Most "mistakes" have a logic to them. Virtually every answer from a child means something. It could mean "I'm bored and not serious." It could mean "I'm trying, but I don't understand." Often, however, the child is following a procedure in his or her mind. It is simply the wrong procedure or the wrong logic by our standard. If we're able, it is far better to figure out the logic and work from there, than simply to label the answer "wrong" and provide the right one.

That great researcher of childhood development, Jean Piaget, taught us that the prekindergarten child doesn't estimate quantity as older children do; the three-year-old brain works differently from the 10-year-old. Five pennies spread across a dinner plate are "more money" than seven clumped together in the middle. A cup of lemonade in a tall thin vase is "more" than after being poured out into a large squat mug.

Abraham Maslow commented once on what people see to be destructiveness in children. "The child who pulls the clock apart is not in his own eyes destroying the clock. He is examining the clock." He is driven by a positive and valuable motive, curiosity.

Maslow universalizes his example. "I am very doubtful that (destructiveness) ever occurs in normal children as a direct primary response to a simple destructive drive. One example after another of apparent destructiveness can be analyzed away dynamically as it is examined more closely."

We do better to ask, "What's going on here?"

Moreover, even using adult reasoning, we grown-ups can be wrong. Twelve-year-old Timmy's interest in cars and in solar energy led him to talk at some length about an automobile that would run on energy from the sun, with solar cells. His father dismissed the idea out of hand, with barely a sentence or two about the very limited currents generated by photo-electric cells. "Impossible!" Fifteen years later, the two of us are exchanging clippings about experimental sunlight-powered cars and the national competition among them. Tim's young logic was fine. How much better, for child/adult sharing and learning, had I but possessed the grace to ask, those years ago, "Tell me how it would work, and what advantages it would have. What are you thinking?"

THERE IS MORE IN TIMING than the developmental concern for what kind of thinking a child can manage at a given age, or what kind of believing, or what level of altruism. Day by day, timing turns out to be a crucial element in our learning.

5. THE APPROPRIATE LEARNING MOMENT

When I was about four, a marble I was playing with rolled into one of the hot air registers that heated our mid-western home. I found I could remove the grate and retrieve my marble, which I did.

A little later that same day, I was running through the house and stepped into the open duct, leaving a painful abrasion on my leg — I had not replaced the grill. At that point my father, who had a good religious library, checked his concordance, sat me down, and read from Proverbs a verse that has stayed with me all my life: "Whoso diggeth a pit shall fall therein." It was an appropriate learning moment.

Had my father read me the Proverbs text two week later and asked, "Do you remember the hot air register?" it would not have stayed with me. Timing is all important.

Learning moments have something almost mysterious to them. Every one of us at one time or another has read a page of interesting material only to find that nothing of it has registered, nothing has sunk in, as we say. At other times we find ourselves virtually devouring the same kind of material with vivid intensity. There is, in fact, an amazingly wide ranging variation in our focus, in the level of attention with which we address ourselves to human experience.

Many of Jesus' parables were evidently first delivered in relation to an event, often one connected to his habit of mixing with the outcasts of his time. As a scribe or Pharisee took him to task or labeled him a blasphemer, then — right then — Jesus told about the Kingdom's erasure of our status system or of a loving parent who sought the dis-enfranchised the way a shepherd would fetch a lost sheep. At Simon's house a woman anointed Jesus' feet with expensive ointment and someone complained. "Simon," said Jesus, "a certain creditor had two debtors..." and he was into a story, capitalizing on a teaching moment.

Such an imaginative freedom to seize the moment characterizes the best teacher. A child brings the story of a dog that has died, and we sit down and speak of how living things die — grandparents included, and we speak of how we can pray to God in trust even then. Another child's baby sister is being baptized, and we take the class to watch, after talking about becoming part of the family of faith, or the baptism of Jesus by John at the Jordan.

It is quite possible that most of our verbal teaching is failing not because it is intrinsicly weak or wrong for the age group at all, but because the timing is off. Watching facial expression and body language, we catch on when the appropriate learning moments come. And we get out of the way when the child — or the adult — plunges into self-directed learning, knowing that the enhanced concentration of the active learner assures maximum absorption of material.

"Whoso diggeth the pit shall fall therein."

QUESTIONS ARE MORE IMPORTANT than answers to the teaching process. Frame a superior question, and you can set a study group off on an hour-long quest of diligent learning. Scientists with the right question can chart a productive research project years long. With the wrong question, they can just as easily waste their time.

6. NO! DON'T ALWAYS NAIL IT DOWN

Overheard in a kindergarten class, one five-year-old to another:

"Do you believe in zero?"

"I believe in zero, but I don't believe in infinity."

These two children were grappling with concepts well over their depths, but they were not talking nonsense. They had in their feelings and in their minds some ideas and attitudes that intrigued them.

Nearing the end of discussion groups and seminars with adults we always used to try nailing down with a summary all the ideas that had been processed. We would write our learnings up on newsprint or on a blackboard. Statements as concise as possible would pull together the concepts and themes that had flowed through the talk lest anyone go away frustrated or having missed the point, feeling it had been a waste of time.

My wife and I still do that sometimes as we lead, but less often. There are advantages in leaving loose ends. Loose ends are invitations to further conversation. They nag at us a little, to keep us thinking and growing. "Do you believe in zero?"

It is a false notion that intelligence consists of propositions ready to be regurgitated, given back to a teacher. Quite the opposite. There is rather a stimulus for intellectual growth — and we use the word for the five-year-olds as well as for adults — in what Leon Festinger calls cognitive dissonance. Cognitive dissonance is the encounter with two mutually contradictory observations or conclusions. One may have a theory of how things "always" work, for example, and then find at least one case in which things do not work that way. Out of such experiences new theories and new ideas are born. We usually resist such maverick observations, even to the point of unconsciously blinding ourselves to them, because they prevent us from "nailing down" answers. They disallow neatness. Important as it is for our sanity that we have some organizing schemes through which to read the world, nailing everything down is deadening.

Religiously, of course, the point is of immense importance. The nearer one approaches to propositionally nailing down a conviction about God — nailing it down in a way that would close off further reflection about this dimension of divine mystery — the more one is going to be wrong about it. "My thoughts are not your thoughts, nor my ways your ways," says the Lord. (Isaiah 55:8)

Wait patiently, therefore, as the children debate their belief in zero. Don't short-cir-cuit the puzzlement with an explanation. Children's wonder takes time. Their quest often has more true intuitive religious sentiment in it than our compulsive explanations have. "A boy's will is the wind's will and the thoughts of youth are long, long thoughts." When it comes to God and things transcendent, we live — praise God — with raveled ends, with partial truths near by, set against the mists of a far horizon.

"LET EVERYTHING THAT has breath praise the Lord." Thus the final chorus in the Psalter ends, after calling on timbrel and trumpet and harp and the dancers, like a good conductor bringing in the horns and tympani. There are psalms of meditative stillness of course, and Elijah's awesome encounter with the still, small voice. But worship in the temple was a noisy affair.

Libraries are properly places of quiet, but for learning the faith, we need not mimic only the stillness of the library or the sanctuary. Learning is a muscular, involving and active affair at its best.

7. LEARNING IS A HAPPENING

My favorite church school teacher one year was Pauline Lagace, who taught our nine-year-old. She reminded me all over again about the secret of teaching and learning — and living. With Pauline, church school became an effervescent "happening."

One day the lesson materials proposed that the class create a litany of praise for good things in this life of ours. "Alleluia" was the suggested response, but to a group that was 85 percent third-grade boys, the word seemed too tame and abstract. A few minutes later, adults at worship heard — echoing through cinder-block walls into the sanctuary — the third-grade celebration of life. First, silence (the first contribution, "for ice cream and hot dogs," was a little tentative), then a loud "Hip, hip hooray!" A pause ("for kites and going fishing"), then "Hip, hip hooray!" Tim remembered that lesson! It was a vivid class hour to him because it was a happening.

When new language surfaces, it usually tells us something significant about the deeper currents of our social experience. "Happening" — as a noun — was new to our vernacular a quarter century ago because on too many occasions, felt the artists and the man or woman on the street, nothing took place. Art was dead, passive. Worship was uneventful. TV created spectators, not participants; "couch potatoes" we were to call them later.

About that worship, incidentally. If Protestant worship has been on the way to renewal, it is in large part because we have been discovering that something takes place in worship. This is not a show we come merely to watch, much less a lecture. We are the ones who make the event by gathering to celebrate together the gospel of God. "The meaning of life was danced out before it was thought out," someone wrote. Here we dance out the Christ Event in the words and actions of the service and the supper — Christ's coming, his teaching, and his self-giving. Preaching becomes a word-event, to use one theologian's words, a rehearsal in which both preacher and people participate.

We can test both worship and teaching with a question, "Is anything happening here?" Are minds growing or changing? Are skills being learned? Some lecturers involve their audiences in eventfulness, but many do not. That is why using debate and discussion, or scattering learners to projects and researches of their own may be better education, even when it seems less concise, less polished.

Christian teaching necessarily requires even more concern for meaningful method than does training in mathematics or carpentry. An invitation to Christian faith is a larger order than the simple transfer of information from one head to another. Revelation — to use a theological term — is more than information. In this process, I am myself changed. I find myself in different relationship to God and my neighbor. Ideally our teaching is one more _event_ in the self-revealing work of God.

A graduate student, frustrated with himself and the process of schooling, put it this way: "I write these papers, hear the lectures, read the books, and get satisfactory marks, but somehow it doesn't _register_ with me."

Our search in Christian education must be for a process that registers. Not every session will have an emotional kick, for learning can be hard, tedious work. But when learning "registers," it is richer and more durable. The "Hip, hip, hooray," we remember hearing as it floated up the stairwell helped both Tim and us grown-ups remember the psalms of praise and take them to heart.

CHAPTER FOUR

TREES

The Church Family

1. A CHILD SHALL LEAD

The church was a normal fellowship of middle-class folk. But that winter the congregation was drifting. Routine had settled in like a darker cloud in an overcast sky. People were stodgy, set in their ways. Worship was uninspiring. An artist in the congregation said that were he to carve it, he would make the worshipers and the pews from a single block, people were so stiff.

But Palm Sunday was coming, and the weather was warmer. The church school children made banners — "Hosanna," "Jesus our King," "Glory in the Highest."

And then the transformation came. Near the end of the service that Palm Sunday, the presiding minister invited everyone to follow the children, during the recessional, out onto the lawn for the final prayers and the benediction.

In a festive mood, while the palm fronds were still being distributed, in came the banner bearers and all the other children with their "branches," parading down the aisle and back out the sides. And the people moved, and sang, and laughed in spite of themselves. It was as if Christ had come into their midst too. Hosanna!

Children in church worship present a larger problem than their restlessness. Far too often the way we "include" them is to put them on display. We in the pews become an audience instead of a congregation praying and worshiping with them. Such displays — in the "children's moment," or even during the junior choir anthem — intrude on the flow of the liturgy. One solution is found in liturgical elements that all ages can do together, children taking lead roles alongside others.

The inclusion strategy takes some imagination. But many churches are on the way. When a family group rather than just children light the Advent candles, we have subtly but importantly transformed the ritual. When the junior choir can sing antiphonally with the adult choir, this is inclusive worship rather than the kiddies' little show. So too, if the lively, syncopated song from the junior high class is used as a teaching occasion. They can help the whole congregation learn a new kind of worship music by inviting folks to join in on the refrain.

We've known for a long time that when lay people read the morning Scripture it helps everyone identify with the reading; it's different from when the pastor does it. Likewise, we can ask a parent and that family's teen to read the two morning lessons. Intergenerational symbols like this emphasize worship by all, youth included. They help show the corporate reality of faith's transmission in families and the family of God.

Another suggestion: We can invite up front for children's stories a few adults from the front pews so they can take part in the conversation or help act a skit with the children. With a few parents joining in for that part of the service, it then makes more sense to give assignments for family prayer, or family research into a Bible story.

One church invites written prayers on a bulletin insert, collected during the offertory, and all are read during the "long prayer" of the service. Prayers that come from children, easily understood as such, are read alongside the others. The congregation's inclusiveness is obvious, and it is a wholesome experience for all worshipers.

We nurture our children in family units far more importantly than in the graded classrooms of the Sunday school, a single hour a week. "Heirs of the covenant," the Bible calls our children, not cherubs on display. One of my life's unforgettables came at an open moment in my daughter's innovative wedding, when worshipers were invited to wish the couple well. The groom's aging Jewish grandfather unexpectedly rose with a patriarchal blessing the equivalent of blind old Isaac's, and then Betsy's 81-year-old maternal (Christian) grandmother did the same. The covenant was tangible that day, and we all became more than mere onlookers at this affair the young folks had planned so well.

The prophet said "A little child shall lead them" when he spoke out his vision of shalom. Helping our children be part of worship instead of performers for us allows into our liturgical life a refreshing spontaneity that can help renew it. In a wonder-filled little book by Dennis Benson and Stan Stewart, The Ministry Of The Child (Abingdon), one of the authors reports on his uneasiness when he visited a terribly dour, conservative congregation in Australia and invited the children to come forward for a special discussion — not the pattern theretofore. His theme was the inclusiveness of the whole church, and the children admitted in conversation that they were all too close in ages to represent the whole church. So Stewart asked each child to go bring an adult forward to join the group. This nice interaction got out of hand, however. After depositing one adult at the front, almost every child went back for another, and another. Soon the whole congregation was standing up front or in the aisles — and enjoying it! New life in the church — from children.

FOLLOWING OUT A RITE OR RITUAL inherited from the past not only binds a people together — a congregation, a family, a nation; it helps us cope with vast and unnerving uncertainties, holding them a little at bay because we believe we're doing the right thing. We can, however, do our rites and rituals compulsively, forgetting their larger purpose. Children bring gifts to the family of God that may redeem well-meant ritual behavior made false by anxieties about what we try to call good order. At least that's what happened in Maple Creek.

2. ALMOND JOY AT OLIVER'S WAKE

Among other things like storytelling and an easy-going manner, Uncle Oliver had been known in his rural Arkansas community for a unique, appealing habit. He converted his own near-addiction to Almond Joy candy bars into a virtue, a vehicle of human relations. Always, he had with him a generous supply, and he gave bars to everyone under 15 whenever he met them. Often enough he gave them to grown-ups too. Child after pony-tailed or freckle-faced child in Maple Creek knew Oliver simply as the man with the Almond Joy.

Oliver's nephew Jamie, age six, was among his favorite consumers, and the ties between Jamie and Oliver had grown fond and strong during Oliver's last brief illness. Jamie even got to walk the six blocks to Oliver's all by himself; he would say he hoped Oliver was better, report on his collection of worms or a bird's nest he found, listen to a story or two, trot back home. Reaching home, he sometimes had not one but two bars of Almond Joy with him.

Now Maple Creek was an unsophisticated place, with unsophisticated churches. People's ways were natural and relaxed enough most of the time. Some events by their nature, however, left the folk of Maple Creek uneasy. Like death. The uneasiness was compounded by a feeling of wanting to do the proper thing but not knowing just how. When Oliver died, full of years, the funeral home people laid him out for a viewing, as the custom was, and the extended family and other friends from Maple Creek gathered in a stiff silence. The dark suits and a good many new-bought neckties were a part of efforts to be proper, as was the hushed quiet of the place, and all the commentary about how nice Oliver looked. But no one really talked much until Jamie paved the way.

Jamie was at the funeral home that night, with his mom and dad, but he found no one else his own age there to talk to. Jamie felt bad about Oliver's passing. He wanted to do something in return for all Oliver had done for him. He also wanted Oliver to be supplied for the trip to Hillside Gardens Cemetary. Finding in his own pocket a left over bar of Almond Joy, courtesy of Uncle Oliver himself, of course, he quietly sidled up to the open casket. He put the bar in Oliver's lapel pocket.

Within minutes, several of Oliver's friends had seen the candy bar, had cried a bit at the tenderness of the gesture, and, in a spirit they could not muster earlier on, had begun to reminisce and talk in loving ways of Oliver. They retold stories and they laughed and cried with each other, easing each other's pain and grief, letting themselves go in affectionate and even boisterous humor. Afterwards, people gave Jamie the credit for breaking open a preoccupation with decorum and making of those visiting hours something very special.

Jesus chose a child as parable once and said God's realm was to be made up of people with gifts like those of children. An unembarrassed trust in life will characterize our faith if we are to follow Jesus — no self-important pretense, no puffed up pride. We are to prize the child in us and not allow it to dry up as we learn the ways of adulthood.

Jamie didn't know the story of the emperor's new clothes, but he broke the ice in Maple Creek that night. He did more. He helped people share the faith that grieves and celebrates a life well-lived when a saint leaves us. Jamie enabled the community to gather together in human sharing and caring that is avenue for the grace of God. All with an Almond Joy.

AMONG THE LIVING who grieve the loss at the time of death are often children and youth. We don't always do them justice as we prepare the funeral or memorial service. Annette tried, and probably succeeded about as well as anyone can, when grief is heavy and a death unfathomable.

3. A CHILDREN'S SERMON AT A FUNERAL?

I wasn't there, but from all accounts it was helpful to the children, and accepted well by the adults — a children's sermon at a funeral service.

Dana's mother had died of cancer. She was 43. Dana was 10. Dana's friends knew Mrs. Bergson not only as Dana's mother. They knew her as one who cared about kids, who was a troop leader for the Girl Scouts, and a community activist in myriad other ways. They wanted to be part of the service, to mourn their loss and Dana's, and to honor a friend and mentor. They would be attending the funeral in considerable numbers.

The young assistant minister had not done this before, and neither had the much older senior. How to include all the children? Annette, the assistant, had read a story to Dana while the extended family had been visiting in the hospital some days before Mrs. Bergson's death. Annette had been caring for Dana apart from the others. At that time she had read her a story: Waterbugs and Dragonflies, (Pilgrim Press, 1982) by Doris Stickney. As simple as it was, it spoke about change, transformation and new life. The senior minister, learning of the rapport between Annette and Dana, asked Annette to do a children's sermon at the funeral in the church. The children's sermon is not a regular feature of Sunday worship at Community Church by any means, but it comes often enough that the "intrusion" seems familiar to many.

Annette, when the moment came, moved out nearer the pews, looked round at the children present, and spoke briefly about loss and grief and about God's care. And she read them Waterbugs and Dragonflies. She then told them how much the story had meant for Dana. Sensing how upset the children were, she also invited them for a long and leisurely conversation in the church's comfortable youth lounge after the service. She felt good about her ministry.

We are told by most pastoral theologians not to exclude children from such important family events as funerals. They mean the children of the family. They suggest little about inclusion of friends and peers of young children. Annette, however, has pioneered a way for us, providing a pattern well worth considering, whichever side one takes in the children's sermon controversy.

LIKE AN ELLIPSE, OUR HUMAN nature has two centers. One is individual; it is our self-consciousness; it provides us freedom within limits set by physiology and by the other center. That second center is social, our participation in the world-beyond-self. The social world, we can justifiably assert, "creates" us in myriad ways, partly establishes character, both setting limits and sustaining us.

We easily overemphasize the first center at the expense of the other as we think of ourselves and of human nature. In church education, for example, we so want youths to choose their faith consciously, to "own" it as we say, that we may forget the social side. Christian faith is a corporate reality as much as it is a personal commitment. The creed says it too. "I believe in (the) church."

4. GIFT OF THE COVENANT

We went to a Bat Mitzvah a while back, the girls' equivalent of the boys' Bar Mitzvah. This was a Sabbath service at a Reformed Jewish temple, and a 13-year-old relative of ours, the candidate, was involved in leading most of the service alongside the rabbi and the cantor.

We were moved by the Bat Mitzvah observance. This recognition of Brenda gave her an identity that would not easily be cast aside during the turbulent years of adolescence that are still ahead. That rootage is particularly important, no doubt, in this child of a mixed marriage. "Am I a Jew or a Methodist, or what?" she must often have asked. The community gathered around her now to take note of her decision.

The service also recognized three years of intensive study. The event celebrated not only Brenda's accomplishment in learning to read a new language but also her ability to do it publicly, and in the context of leading communal worship.

One striking and important feature of the service was the gentle but clear reiteration that this step marked Brenda's entrance into the full life of the congregation as an adult. As an adult certain privileges and responsibilities were hers, one of the first being that of participant/reader in Friday night service two weeks hence. Brenda would participate not as guest or "youth representative," but with the sense of permanent ownership of this new identity and all the dignity conferred with it.

We were especially touched at one point in the service, and we pondered how to learn from it for our own rites of confirmation. After the dramatic moments of removing the Torah from its ark and the "test" when young Brenda did her reading of the scheduled Sabbath portion, there was a ceremony of blessing. Brenda's mother and father were invited to the podium, and grandparents from both sides too. Her parents then placed their hands on Brenda's shoulders while the rabbi gave the blessing, his hands, meanwhile, on her head. It was a passing on of a family mantle; it was Isaac's blessing given to Jacob; it was the Shema's command being fulfilled again: "You shall teach them (the commandments) diligently to your children."

Talking on the way home, we pondered two major elements in our confirmation emphases in Protestant Christianity, and how one gets lost — an important one — in our concern for the other. Out of our evangelical roots, we are deeply concerned that our young people and all Christians do more than inherit a pro forma faith. We want them to "own" a personal religious experience, a personal commitment to the God we have been blessed to know in Jesus Christ. But do we so center our confirmation on that necessary experience that we neglect another element for our confirmands — the acknowledgement of a history and tradition and covenant into which they are moving, a covenant mediated by both congregation and parents?

This rite of passage does contribute to an identity apart from parents, to be sure. That is one of our goals for adolescence. But would it not be strengthened, rather than diminished, by involving the parents in the giving of a blessing?

Our Puritan forebears were much more a people of the Old Testament than we are. Conceivably, they may have underplayed, until the days of the Awakenings and the revivals, this evangelical element we so stress. But they knew about the covenant, "even to the third and fourth generations." In these days of such troubled adolescence, of emotionalism and self-centeredness, had we not better recover a stronger sense that, even when parental religious participation is shallow, a confirmand claims a heritage as well as a personal faith?

Someone will ask, "But what about the broken homes and the dislocated children living apart from natural parents altogether?" (My parish's youth group started off the season last fall with eight teens, five of them from single-parent homes.) So much the more important, perhaps, to strengthen what home and heritage there is, rather than hiding these painful realities beneath the veil of "sensitivity."

And what of the parents whose own participation in the religious community has been more honored in the breach? Every confirmation class seems to produce at least one puzzling and puzzled candidate whose parents' sole involvement consists of delivering and fetching the confirmand-to-be. Still one must assume that even such perfunctory religiosity bears witness to some unnamed yearnings for connection. The connection goes back in time to a broader history, as well as inward toward the hungering hunches of God's grace. One implies the other in our Trinitarian faith; our God creates all that is, redeems us through Israel's story and its culmination in the Christ-Event, and remains our contemporary in the sustaining, sanctifying presence of the Spirit.

Let's consider having the parents participate in the blessing, and consider somehow using the language of an ancient covenant to give more body to our own confirmation rites. The new member receives covenant from and joins in with a vast cloud of witnesses, past and present.

IF THE FORMATION of newcomers ingrafted to the church depends so heavily upon the congregation, and if the reality of God's people lives in congregations as they shape and react with our Christian individuality, the church educator and church parent have more work to do than organizing classes in which information is handed out to well-disciplined youngsters. The educator and conscientious parent are concerned for the life of the whole church for educational reasons, let alone all the others.

5. BEYOND THE SUNDAY SCHOOL

Define the educational task to be fostering growth in understanding of and commitment to the Christian life. There follows the correlate fact that all kinds of activity within parish life have educational significance. Church educators need to relate their specific responsibilities to the educational dimensions of parish life, dimensions that go well beyond the Sunday school. Given imagination and sensitivity, educators and church school administrators can enhance the ministry of their congregations by sparking many educational activities outside the formal teaching sector. Christians were nurtured and taught long before there were Sunday schools!

Item. After an embarrassingly "bad" funeral, one church board charged with oversight in pastoral care decided to begin planning a leaflet that would help people at the time of a death in the family to arrange a more meaningful funeral or memorial service. Their discussion led them into a much wider range of issues than they had expected, and a sub-committee found itself over several months leading the full board in a learning adventure. Their areas of concern included the reality of grief, definitions of faith and hope and resurrection, issues of sentimentality and integrity and meaning in face of death, theological questions about the phrase, "the will of God." They spoke about their own views of death and the issue of heroic (and costly) medical measures that prolong the life of the body when mind and spirit are gone. Their work led to a longer leaflet than they had envisioned, including a record of funeral requests to be filed with the church office, and a suggested "living will" about those heroic measures, applicable should one leaving such a will become comatose. They spoke of stewardship and legacies and benevolence. In short, this committee's routine work became a long-term educational and service project that affected in one way or another nearly every family in the congregation.

Education, the learning-teaching activity of intentional growth in knowledge, skill and inner understanding is or can be a dimension of most activity in the congregation, not simply the Sunday school and adult study classes. Ancient prayers and traditions of the church year are introduced for Advent, Epiphany and Lent, let's say, with the bulletin carrying information about their origins. A series of sermons goes exegetically through one of the prophets in the context of Old Testament history, or even through the tough life-and-death issues of contemporary medical ethics, all the while speaking from the perspective of Godward faith, so that they are still sermons, not lectures. During the course of a year, one church worshiped with carefully researched services out of half a dozen climes and times — a Geneva order under Calvin, a colonial New England church meeting (with abbreviated sermon!), a high Wesleyan canon for the liturgy, a hymn-singing revival from the frontier. This was experiential learning at its best and it fostered growth in ecumenical consciousness as well.

With little doubt, one of the least used but potentially richest possibilities for wider education in most churches is the use we make of church music. Most church choirs rehearse week after week without taking a moment to reflect on the texts and the musicology of what they sing. What is the biblical context of Isaiah's "Comfort ye?" Why does the composer shift to the minor and a quiet mood at this point in the psalm? How legitimate is this contemporary text as an expression of Christian grief or joy? How well does this piece express the presence of Christ we know in the Eucharist? We need two kinds of "warm-up" to make our music better and to help us grow — the "ma-me-mi-mo-mu" exercises for the voice, but also the theological reflection before we sing. Much the same can also be said of teaching and learning new hymns in the whole congregation.

One of my favorite candidates for getting education out of the corner into all the church is the bell choir. Bell choirs are coming to symbolize the church at its best for me. Well-trained, they glorify God superbly as they provide prelude or offertory in worship. Well-directed, they help amateurs learn to enjoy the learning process. But most of all, well-recruited, they pull together an age-range of participants that is unique among social groupings these days outside a family reunion. Our choir has had in it a seven-year-old and a 79-year-old, making music together, with most of the decades in between being represented too. That's education and grafting into the whole community of faith. Rehearsals are something of a weekly reunion for God's family, like worship itself.

CHAPTER FIVE

Nutrients

1. DEAR JEFF

My daughter and son-in-law built their first home way back in the Appalachian hills of West Virginia. With their own hands they built it, helped by a few relatives and college chums pitching in sporadically on their summer vacations. It was a lovely, lovely place hidden in a valley with just enough flatland to support a few cows and pigs and chickens, a small apple orchard and a garden that changed year by year toward what I call dirt from the clay and sand base that they began with.

When their older children were five and three years old, they still had not found an adequate nearby church. They had been driving 50 miles for church when they could make it. With mixed hope and uneasiness, they started up a little home-based Sunday school for the people in their cove: "two Catholic families, one Southern Baptist, one Methodist, and us."

It is a literalist, fundamentalist environment in the hills of West Virginia and the way the Bible stories are being told in this new Sunday School had this young couple on edge. "The things they have covered, far too literally for me," wrote Jeff, "include Noah's ark and the flood and the creation story." Then he goes on, "Rereading these, I was again horrified at the violence, the demeaning position of women, and the wrathful and vengeful nature of God. How do you feel about this kind of biblical history?"

Dear Jeff,

I appreciate your worry about what a literalist reading and retelling of those old Bible stories may mean to Abigail and Sarah. You are well-educated people — one of you in biology and one in educational psychology — with a fine liberal arts background, so the foolishness of reading the classic yarns of Genesis as literal history is apparent to you. But please don't let that put you off. Stick with the group. I have but four simple points in response to the uneasiness in your good letters.

1) Children are amazingly resilient little persons when they come from a home as secure and supportive as yours is. The stories are told them by some in your group in

very literalist terms, but that is how children of Sarah and Abigail's ages have to think anyway. With the discussions you yourselves are also having with the children, I have no doubt that later on as these stories are remembered, God will evolve for them into something less literally old-man-and-beard than at present. Although at least one writer/scholar wants us to postpone all talk about God until children are 12, because before that Godtalk is heard by them in such concrete pictures, I see no way that we can do that in a culture like ours. Let the children hear interpretation from the literalist Christians and also from you, realizing that you have a far larger impact on your kids at home than has half a morning at Sunday school.

2) Stories are part of our culture, and Bible stories are an essential part of our religious culture. How can we talk about passover and baptism and even Easter without the story of the Red Sea exodus from Egypt? How can we understand Matthew's and Luke's story about Jesus' 40 days in the desert without remembering the 40 years in the wilderness? If we are to speak of a God who, in spite of human struggle and pain, in spite of our loss and grief, promises us grace and peace, how could we leave out as part of the background the lore of Noah and the rainbow promise, and the dynamism of the covenant with Abraham? Those covenant promises have sustained the Jews as a people through pogrom and holocaust and yet untold more anguishes beyond all recording. How could we interpret the nature and destiny of human being in a purposeful creation, which is our faith, without something like those various stories of Creator and creation so beautifully condensed in Genesis 1 and Genesis 2? Let the lore be shared, in bedtime story and even by those literalists of your Sunday school.

3) About the violence, again remember the corrective gift of your home and the resilience of children. Remember too that violence is nothing so new to children. Violence is even nearby. Always, I think, I shall remember Abigail's protest to you, when it was butchering time, about "Mr. Brown," the cow she had named, when you tried to comfort her with some comment about how sad it is that things have to die. "But Mr. Brown didn't just die; you killed him," she said. Age 3! You won't play up the violence, of course. I pray your fundamentalist friends don't either. But it's in the American Revolution Sarah will learn about in the fourth grade, and it's in the Bible too. They were violent times when David and Saul faced the Philistines and when Jesus was crucified by the Roman authorities. There's no hiding place from that kind of world until we grown-ups can do a better job of discovering there's neither Jew nor Greek in the community of God. And the lore of the Bible, even if taught in such a questionable context as yours, seems likely to have a place in building towards that day.

4) Your part in that Sunday school will have an impact, I'm sure, in spite of how outnumbered you feel. For the time being, at least, stay with it and build some bridges with your literalist Christian friends. If they rule you out, so be it, but your faith is as authentic as theirs, and you are all trying to pass on something marvelously good and important to your children.

Keep writing, and good luck with the Sunday school adventure.

Love,
Dad

IN SPITE OF LIP SERVICE insisting on the importance of the Bible, assumptions about Scriptural authority vary widely in the church. The following article put into a twiggy nutshell a reaction to this diversity. A temptation toward fundamentalism arises as a reaction to unnervingly rapid social change in any institution or as a repression of personal malaise. Fundamentalism is neither very biblical nor very profound as an expression of faith or even an assertion of biblical authority. Faith in the midst of change is far deeper than insistence on textual rigidities. "Though the earth do change," wrote the Psalmist, confident in the midst of social upheaval, God's steadfast love endures. Moreover, literalism of itself provides inadequate guidance in appropriating the Bible as ground for living. Are we to give equal weight to the dietary laws of Leviticus and Paul's ad hoc admonition that "Women should not speak in church" and to the sixth commandment? Are we really to treat in the same fashion the creation accounts, the drama of Job, a Gospel's story of Jesus and the epic of the Spirit in the book of Acts?

Yet, clearly our Christian interaction with Scripture rests on firmer foundations than a merely antiquarian or literary interest in some ancient religious writings.

2. THE CHURCH EDUCATOR AND THE BIBLE

How are we to use the Bible if we are to both undergird its importance and understand it more deeply than thinking it a confusing source of proof-texts? The question plagues the beginning educator of kindergartner's and "chronologically gifted" alike.

First, I believe we acknowledge the formative power of language. The "language" of the church is the Bible. Language forms community. It provides common thought patterns, shared meanings and commitments. Biblical material offers us images and metaphors for reflection at the various depths of insight that different people have, the way good poetry does. Think of the prodigal son, the way of the cross, the tower of Babel, or Creation and Fall as expressions for our human situation in the God-relation. They all say more, to more people, in much smaller and more powerful compass than propositional theological argumentation.

In our learning community in the church, therefore, we use the biblical imagery as often as appropriately possible. Our good hymns and religious folk songs use biblical language. We tell the Bible stories — repeatedly — as ways of enriching the storehouse of communication and soul-shaping. The community we build covers time as well as space, for this language — as contrasted to the "pop" idiom of the faddish moment — was used by Christians long before our time and will be for centuries to come. We are a people rooted in memory and hope, continuities sustained by the Bible.

The Bible in Christian experience has also proven to be surpassingly a book of devotion. We do not read the lessons in church as mere "thoughts for the day" or texts for the sermon. The reading is also a liturgical action, pointing to and reciting the story of God's saving action for us. We sing and read the psalms as prayers of the human spirit in this age-old community — in celebration and penitence and grief. We read the passion narratives and the parables and epistles as devotional literature of the God-relation as much or more than ground for cognitive learning. The Bible, as both a multi-faceted and a normative expression of the God-relation, prompts in us both the intention and the ability to live in that God-relation for ourselves.

There are other perspectives — by the shelf-full, on the power of Scripture in Christian life and history. Here is the literary production of a whole people's encounter with God, history and poetry, drama and gospel, epistle and vision — of cosmic beginnings and apocalypse. So strong and so deep is this material, and so significant for a whole people, that we call it revelation, or word of God. Or we say we find God's Word through these words. Here Christ speaks to us so movingly in word and deed and sacrifice that we call the book a living document though it is an ancient text. No wonder that some become attached to its every word and resist the scholars who fulfill their proper role with technical criticism. No wonder too that we still acknowledge its mystery, even as we rejoice in dedicated scholarly insights.

Bound together with this common language, praying its prayers and rehearsing its narrative in sacrament and word, we discover the Bible working its way with us. The Bible's main authority with God's people has always claimed and shaped us by this subtle route more than by the debates evoked among us because we have such differing points of view on how to interpret its writings.

ANOTHER QUESTION about what we feed our twigs and trees has to do with character formation and moral behavior. Frustrated by accounts of corruption and violence in the media, and imputing moral decline to the whole social order, people say to the church, "Why don't you teach them morals?"

The hard reality is that you and I don't mainly nourish our trees with direct intravenous injection. It's all roundabout. We water the roots, clear the way for sunshine, put fertilizer down, spread mulch around.

We use an indirect means to achieve moral character as well.

3. WHY DON'T YOU TEACH THEM MORALS?

"Why don't you teach them morals?" Speaking to the advisor of her son's youth group, a frustrated parent has two worries on her mind.

In a nearby "Bible chapel" there is a fast-growing youth club and a no ifs-ands-or-buts style of teaching right and wrong. Moreover, Mrs. Jamison feels that her own son is unchallenged by either the "fun and games" — as she calls them — or the serious discussions in the youth group at her own church.

"Teaching morals" in a pluralistic society frustrates not only parents and public school teachers. It frustrates advisors of church youth as well. An authoritarian, sect-like mentality tempts us in spite of our better judgment.

Or is it our better judgment, we ask. We wonder if stricter teaching, which avoids stubborn moral ambiguities by saying certain things are always right and others absolutely wrong might not be a better way — at least for teenagers.

Two things must be said to Mrs. Jamison's credit. She is concerned. And she knows the purpose of a church youth group is more than fun and games. Leaders of youth are often unclear about their goals in fellowship activity. They know the group is not a class, or a congregation at worship. So some advisors end up feeling that a "good group" is enough. Mrs. Jamison knows better.

But what about "teaching morals?" How does that process take place?

The ambiguity in moral education by the church arises from two principles to which Christians pay serious respect. First, Christian faith at its center is not a set of moral rules spelled out like so many embellishments on the Ten Commandments. Our faith provokes in us profoundly moral concerns and we are given by God's grace a Way, a Torah. But, instead of a restricting law, we Christians know a liberating joy in the God we meet through Christ.

St. Paul went so far in his experience of legalistic religious interpretation as to say "the law is dead." Freedom in Christ creates in us a loyalty to God and a commitment to neighbor-love that seriously probes the questions of justice and personal virtue. Hence Mrs. Jamison's passion for right teaching. But the Bible is more of a storybook about

God's way with us than it is a cookbook of rules for proper behavior. It is through our celebration of the story that Christians are made whole by God's grace rather than through the personal virtues we cook up from the rules.

Secondly, we know that moral character is a quality of persons, not a function of machines. If we have much sense, we do not aim at programming our children and youth for automatic reflexes that make them perform in flat "moral" patterns of routine respectability. Rather, we want them to be loving, creative persons with an inner freedom showing through in a zest for life. That means taking the risk of less respectability and traditional piety for the sake of a richer walk with God and neighbor.

The scholar Lawrence Kohlberg, who analyzed moral development in youth and adulthood, argued that the fully mature person holds to a pattern of integrity not for fear of punishment or of disapproval from others, or of losing a reward, but from an inner conviction that is simply the good to which he or she is committed. ("I couldn't live with myself if I did that," a mature person might say.)

Many, many adults never mature that far, of course. They find their motivation for moral behavior in laws and in the disapproval of others. Implicitly, when such people can do for their own advantage what is unjust or deceitful without danger of punishment or disapproval, they will. They may be so relativistic in their own thinking indeed that their basic definition of the right and good rests only on what is expedient for their self-interest as long as punishment can be avoided. They do not reflect seriously on what is simply right or just or true, or, to put it another way, on God's hope for the human community.

Moral reasoning depends on an ability to recognize the difference between private desire and moral obligation, between my personal wants and a more objectively described rightness or goodness that can lay claim on me. St. Paul exhibited that ability when he wrote that he could "will the good" but that he found himself doing evil because of his own selfish inclination.

All this says something important to the Mrs. Jamison in each of us. If we aim for moral maturity, our style in family life, church education and youth activities will be structured to include a strong sense of selfhood and responsible relations to others. This is a much broader, more deeply moral goal than proper obedience to a set of societal or religious rules. We call it character.

Kohlberg reports that strong bonds of trust with parents and other mentors lead to moral maturity in youth more because they promote "Ego Identity" and internally secure persons than because of direct right-and-wrong indoctrination from the mentors.

Maturity is correlated with competence for inner moral judgment and not with stronger law-and-order anxieties. Merely enforcing rules that one kind of church or one kind of school teacher proclaims as the laws of God forcloses active moral reflection and practice in decision making. It leaves open the possibility of retarded moral development or of moral cynicism, should the student come later to question these particular "Godly" rules.

These insights into moral development do not prompt good leaders to play the role of a non-partisan on moral issues. We need parents and teachers and youth advisors of character and of passionate conviction. However, the perspective does mean that promoting unthinking obedience is almost the very opposite of teaching morality to our youth.

This approach assists us with a related bogy word, indoctrination. The word evokes images of authoritarians and brain-washing. And there is bad indoctrination of that sort. The word, however, should not scare us off. Small children need to be indoctrinated in many ways simply on our own authority. But good indoctrination, good teaching of morals, gives rules with reasons. It gives the reasons as early as a child's maturity and comprehension allow, so that moral understanding and character can follow.

Mrs. Jamison is right about fun and games groups in which leaders do not provoke thoughtful discussion of justice and generosity, what is right and what is good. Reflection that leads to moral commitment is one of the most characteristically human and spiritually essential activities we know. But Mrs. Jamison is wrong if she thinks teaching morals means merely rote learning of ethical do's and don'ts whether a person is 15 or 50.

AT NINE, CHRIS LEARNED AND LOVED BIBLE STORIES for their own sake, without much concern for the factuality of Noah's ark or the seven days of creation. At 12 Chris pondered the seriousness with which people took these stories and wondered what to make of written and television accounts of evolution, or scientific law that seemed violated in a miracle. Chris was typical in his development. "Did the sun really stand still?" he asked when his class was working on a time-line and his part was to study the conquest of Canaan.

Many a college sophomore could have been spared a crisis of faith — sometimes long-term in duration — had he or she been given better answers to questions like that in church school.

4. CREATION *AND* EVOLUTION AT OUR CHURCH PLEASE

Hundreds of children and their parents from miles around flocked to a "beheading and re-heading" of a famous dinosaur skeleton a while back in our city's natural history museum. Scholars had decided the immense frame had been fitted with the wrong skull fragments!

Ancient and extinct species hold a strange fascination for us and our children. The dinosaur craze, at least, shows few signs of abating, even yet.

This fascination probably accounts in some measure for the publicity given the "scientific creationists," who believe that as a scientific theory of origins, evolution is wrong. Gathering enough strength, this small group even forced some textbook revisions for a while. Creationists say the earth is much younger than the scientific community at large would have it, and that new species, rather than coming about through evolutionary change, spring up suddenly by divine fiat.

Rather than dismiss the creationists out of hand, we do well to reflect on the naivete and personal anxieties that underlie their point of view. The science-and-religion issue stays with us generation after generation, dinosaur fossils and paleontologists notwithstanding.

Begin with the scraps of truth behind the creationists' concerns. If science is so taught as to imply that it can be our messiah, providing not only food and power enough, miracle drugs, and a thousand life-sustaining comforts but also the saving, root meaning for our lives, then science is very poorly taught. Science does not determine ultimate hope and the norms of justice, goodness and beauty. It cannot save itself.

Science is basically descriptive. "This is how things appear to work," it says. "This is how the world appears to have begun and changed. This is how the species appear to have arisen." However, to mix religious and moral categories into this reporting, explaining through "science" the ultimate meaning of these sequences, is to go beyond the realm of science.

The long tradition of scientific work in observation and experimentation, of course, provides science, especially in the case of the natural sciences, with immense predictive powers as well. Otherwise we could have never paid a human visit to the moon. Science, however, did not of itself make the decision to head moonward; that was a societal choice, a matter of moral decision.

Scientific creationists have heard about teaching that, in the name of science, makes claims outside that realm. They themselves, however, react from an equally confused set of categories. They transform the marvelous myths of origin in Christian lore, stories that are fundamentally poetic and religious, into sources for paleontology, geology and biology. While claiming scientific authority, somehow, for them, God must work in a particular way in creation, or else God is not fully God. It seems to them that God must intervene from outside a system, creating the human species, for example, de novo. That God works through the very evolutionary process which science approaches descriptively, seems beyond their ken.

We deal here, of course, with perennial and profound issues of meaning in religious language. Even to say "God works" this way or that way illustrates the point. Inevitably, our language limits God. It makes God separate and apart, while God is also the empowering ground of things. "In God we live and move and have our being."

Church educators need to have pondered these matters whether they teach children of six or 60. Science is a tool, for which we speak our gratitude to God. The tool challenges us to make choices about how to use it. Because we are able to mass produce weapons does not mean we must make them or use them.

The tool uncovers natural processes from the intra-nuclear level to that of inter-galactic space, and our awe in face of that may feed religious sensibilities. Science of itself, again, tells us next to nothing about whether the universe should be interpreted as purposive or an amazing clockwork signifying nothing.

In our classrooms with learners of all ages, we are to celebrate our human curiosity and competence as evidenced in science. We celebrate, however, in relation to these higher sensibilities. We will show pleasure in our students' fascination with dinosaurs and space-ships and black holes, at babies being born, or Siamese twins being given separate life. We have no quarrel with legitimate descriptions of evolution, and the intellect's predictive endeavors, with medicine's ability to alleviate human suffering. We urge these uses of science.

We participate as Christians, however, in public debate and decision-making about what to do with the knowledge science brings us. These moral matters — whether to build more nuclear power or create more test-tube babies — are concerns far broader than those of the experimenters. The creationists are right to be up in arms if they know teachers who narrow such concerns to "science." A child's report on a dinosaur beheading invites significant talk in any classroom. The implications offer content for a whole teachers' meeting too.

5. CHRISTIAN EDUCATION IN THE NINETIES: PREDICTION/PRESCRIPTION

Looking into the nineties as church educators, we can ask what is likely to happen, or we can ask what ought to. Prediction is not the same as prescription!

A denominational executive bent on creating new forms of mission said once, "The parish church as we know it simply won't exist 10 years from now!" That was almost 30 years ago! The bureaucrat's prescriptive enthusiasm had weakened his predictive competence.

Future-thinking is complex for another reason. Sometimes someone predicts "A" as a threat. Then people heed prediction and bring about "B" instead of "A." The predictor is proven wrong!

Sometimes a prophet resents that. Nineveh repented when Jonah predicted God's judgment. So God had a change of heart, which "displeased Jonah exceedingly and he was angry" (Jonah 4:1).

First, some predictions, but briefly... It's the prescriptions that really challenge our creativity, and if, being followed, they falsify the predictions, so much the better.

1. In all probability, Sunday schools will continue to be standard fare in most congregations. They have proven to be durable, and what's left of protected time for religious activity is still on Sunday morning.

2. Adult education will continue too — with fellowship, spiritual growth, and cognitive inquiry being the motivators for considerable Sunday learning in the Bible belt and for fewer but significant weeknight and weekday learning groups — some on-going, many short-term — all over the country and across most denominations. Non-denominational, informal Bible study and even academically formal, post-high theological education among the laity will expand, especially among the retired.

3. Experimentation will continue. Here a new curriculum will enliven an educational enterprise; there a new video tool will catch the imagination. Here a new tie-in to the lectionary and liturgical year will bind together the generations in a congregation the way the "international lessons" did for our great-grandparents; there a midweek all-church learning event will survive the onslaughts of secular culture.

All these things are good. They have the strength of tradition and viability. They nurture people in the faith and have enormous potential for doing more.

II

What <u>prescriptions</u> would one make for the nineties? As Christians we prescribe in response to both Gospel imperative and changing social realities.

Each of my prescriptions responds to social change that is hurting our educational success at present or challenging us to greater depth and breadth in our educational work.

1. <u>Teaching in a global context</u>. "Planet earth" consciousness must affect our teaching content and style. From an early age, children must now think of social reality in multi-racial terms, of moral reality as a struggle on the world community's part toward justice for the poor, of physical reality with profound ecological consciousness, and of inter-religious reality as dialogue rather than Christian triumphalism. Sensitive, theologically grounded teaching will have new horizons in the nineties.

2. <u>More professional leadership</u>. The continual sophistication of the post-industrial society means that for most middle class churches amateurism in guiding the educational enterprise doesn't suffice. People with educational TV on their cable, a college degree in their history, and professionals around them at work are not content with Bible stories of David and Goliath or simplistic slogans about Christ being the answer to every dilemma. Like Jacob, they are ready to wrestle for their blessing.

Educational leaders needn't be ordained, or paid in every case, but they need theological education as well as organizational and pastoral interpersonal competence. And they should be continually at work with this theological substance, educating their teaching staff and doing direct adult education with others as well. In small parishes, the pastor's self-understanding must include a self-conscious role as church educator.

Theologically alert volunteers can be found for this work in many congregations, even people with graduate degrees in religion. Nurture them. If the status of professional church educators is better supported by pastoral attitude and church pay scales, we can achieve a renewal of our church education. Public educators are now much better recognized than 10 years ago; it's time for the church to follow suit.

This upgrading needn't always mean new personnel. Thousands of churches are within commuting distance of an acceptable seminary in which they can sponsor advanced study by their present educational leaders.

3. <u>Intensive growth experiences</u>. Out-of-town week-ending and other marks of a highly mobile society challenge us to patterns that go beyond our reliance on week-in, week-out continuity in Sunday morning classrooms. Like summer conferences, adult and teenage learning retreats, perhaps six times a year, can accomplish as much as weekly hour-long sessions. Regular, extended midweek gatherings (5 to 9 p.m. with dinner, for example), for fellowship and learning, make compelling sense when Sunday absenteeism can reach 50 percent.

Some mainline churches have succeeded in reversing the sleep-in trend by making Sunday mornings much more important and eventful. Try an all-church weekly breakfast and seminar for all ages, or, for the down town church, a weekly "lunch and learning" session for all. When there are children in the area, and overly hassled single parents or uninterested ones, try the church-bus pattern again.

4. <u>Technology</u>. The easy use of video cassettes, replacing the awkward, noisy fuss of 16 millimeter films, can transform much of our teaching. A church should be building a library of videos, adding in some of its own devising. Lively educational tools can be made from interviews with other religious leaders in town (rabbis and even Muslims and Buddhists included, in many cities), oral history from old-timers, well-edited lectures by visiting missionaries, theologians or social action leaders. Let such tools always be used along with discussion and reflection; Christian education has deeper goals than accumulating facts in our heads.

5. <u>Learning by going</u>. An affluent society and inexpensive travel provide us more learning avenues. One single church I know has taken a 12-member adult seminar on a study of South African apartheid and Christian missions, and a similar group of teens and adults to an Indian reservation work-camp 1400 miles away. Lasting interests and friendships have resulted. Elder hostels and denominational tours already sponsor studies of religious history, spirituality, international justice, Bible lands. We need to make education a happening, taking our learners to interview religiously concerned pro-life and pro-choice people at a picket line, going to work down the street at a Habitat for Humanity project or in the soup kitchen. "Why poverty?" questions then take on urgency. Let there be more learning by going in the nineties.

<u>A final word</u>: The foundational assumptions for renewed Christian education in the nineties include an ongoing conviction that such learning is urgent and valuable, that the worshiping congregation is at the heart of church life, that biblical faith is to be nurtured even in discussions that lack explicit biblical content, and that Christian education is uniquely invitational rather than merely pedagogical. In all our work, we are inviting people to Christian commitment as well as study.

6. SANDCASTLES

We can work too hard on believing, forgetting it is ultimately God's gift and not our own achievement. Christian faith is not a process of laying one course of stone and brick upon another until the foundations are in place, the doors are set, the plumbing and roof complete. Even while we build we ask over and over again, "Is faith possible?" Paul warned us when he said, "The wisdom of this world is folly with God."

Spending some time on a summer's beach watching children may help us. Jesus' words sustain us in the watching, "Unless you turn and become like children, you will never enter the realm of God's governance."

Childlikeness is often taken to imply an innocent sense of awe. But that is not the whole story. Take a longer look at the children and reflect on the lightheartedness that is part of what Jesus means when he says children are the ones who inherit the kingdom.

The children are not so awestruck by the sunset at the beach. It is the people over 30, over 60, who watch the sun go down. The children scurry back and forth, picking up stones and hurling them into the waves. They busy themselves with sandcastles. The adults watch the sun and talk.

Sandcastles are a clue to our work in life and our work at faith. They are not intended to justify anyone's existence, to transform the world, to participate in any revolution, to be permanent memorials to wisdom. They suffer a magnificent, apocalyptic end when the waves break on shore after the evening calm. But the children build them with a transfixed seriousness.

Their play is a kind of work. Their work is this play. In spite of imminent destruction, they build seriously. The children seem to know it won't really matter ultimately. And their patient, passionate work is laced with joy.

We cannot accuse the children of cynicism as they build these short-lived castles. They know as well as we that it is preposterous to expect a sandcastle to be a lasting monument. They accept the gift of sand and shore and work with it, diligently, and with an interior grace.

We are utterly serious in our question for faith and in our reforming activism. But we walk a dead-end street if we do not allow for a certain lightheartedness as we work. The sign of the cross makes it clear that we cannot expect our work to justify us. Our work is not equipped for that. We may lift a quizzical eyebrow and ask of our own proud work, "Is this a sandcastle too?" It is.

This work of ours, at faith, at life, is a gift. Strange as it sounds, we can take this work so seriously we forget that faith comes at its own pace alongside, not in increments as we set one course of bricks upon another.

The secular moralist asks, when we talk this way, "But don't you cut the nerve of action if you separate the gift of God from the earnest enterprise of building? Don't you belittle all the virtues in human achievement, in zealous service to the race, and all learning? If what we build does not persist because of its own worth in the divine commonwealth, what, then, is worth working on?"

Our answer could be historical. Those most emphatic as to God's overwhelming sovereignty have also been activists. But the secularist shows us humanists who work as hard. We could tell the secularist that moral action wrongly motivated is as bad as no action at all. But he will prove us wrong.

We do better to speak of the freedom with which a person can work if able to sit a little loose to that work. Without working compulsively, we work better.

That is the principle way there can be art in work, and the only way there can be hope left when the waves come up after the evening calm. And it makes our towers of Babel into temples of the Spirit.

This is the freedom that sings with Luther, "Let goods and kindred go," because it knows God's more enduring love. Children give us enormous hope sometimes as we look with them at their future, but seeing them build their dripcastles in the sand intimates an even more ultimate and hope-filled grace.